John Oldham

Twayne's English Authors Series

Bertram H. Davis, Editor

Florida State University

TEAS 372

JOHN OLDHAM
(1653–1683)
Photograph courtesy of
The Newberry Library. Chicago. Illinois

John Oldham

By James Zigerell

Twayne Publishers   •   Boston

John Oldham

James Zigerell

Book Production by John Amburg

Book Design by Barbara Anderson

Printed on permanent/durable acid-free
paper and bound in the United States of
America.

Library of Congress Cataloging in
Publication Data

Zigerell, James.
    John Oldham.

    (Twayne's English authors series ; TEAS 372)
    Bibliography: p. 139
    Includes index.
    1. Oldham, John, 1653–1683—Criticism and
interpretation.   I. Title.   II. Series.
PR3605.04Z98   1983   821'.4   83–10722
ISBN 0–8057–6858–0

245643

For Rosamond and Joan

Contents

About the Author

James Zigerell received the A.B. and A.M. degrees from Loyola University in Chicago, and the Ph.D. from the University of Chicago. He was Professor of English and Humanities at Wright College of the City Colleges of Chicago and Lecturer in English at Loyola.

His doctoral dissertation was on the novels of Samuel Richardson. He is also interested in modern literature. A long-time reviewer of poetry, fiction, and critical studies for *Choice* and other journals, he has contributed articles on contemporary poetry and fiction to *The Explicator* and *Twentieth Century Literature*, as well as to *The Journal of Aesthetic Education* and other journals.

At present he is involved in encouraging colleges and universities to make use of the mass media, especially television, in extending formal and informal instruction. He serves as a consultant on televised instruction to a number of professional organizations and higher education institutions.

He and his wife live in Glenview, Illinois.

Preface

If they know him at all, most students of English literature know John Oldham, the subject of this study, only through snippets in collections of seventeenth-century verse or through John Dryden's touching memorial verses written on the occasion of his early death. Dryden's memorial, "To the Memory of Mr. Oldham," does, by the way, do much more than pay tribute to a gifted young man snatched away too early. It provides a balanced assessment of his merits and faults as a poet—not surprising from one who was a superb critic.

The purpose of this study is to introduce someone unacquainted with Oldham to an original and vigorous satiric voice of Restoration England, a period marked by acrimonious political and religious controversies and divisions. For the reader to whom Oldham's work is not unknown, the study, it is hoped, will provide an overview of his achievement and place him in proper perspective.

Oldham, who died in 1683 while only thirty, was in his creative years at a time when king, court, Parliament, Catholic, Whig, and Tory were objects of the most bitter vituperation in print and, in cases where the attacks would surely have run afoul of the Licensing Act, in unpublished manuscripts that made the rounds of the coffee-houses. Even though, as an Oxford scholar, he was a loyal king's man, Oldham made a reputation during his brief career as an eloquent and resourceful enemy of the forces he saw as intent on depriving freeborn Englishmen of their liberties and returning the country to the tyranny of popery.

Thus, in the blazing propaganda of the *Satires Upon the Jesuits,* he exploited to the full the hysteria and frenzy surrounding the "discovery" of the Popish Plot on the life of the king. The mysterious and intrepid Jesuits who, at the risk of horribly cruel punishment and death, left their seminaries on the Continent and, pledged to support the Pope, slipped into England both to minister to those who had clung to the old faith and to work toward restoring the realm to the Old Church, served his purposes as the very embodiment of treachery and duplicity. Making the nation even more receptive to Oldham's vehement attack on the company of Loyola was the prospect of an avowed Roman Catholic, James, the Duke of York, succeeding his brother Charles II, who remained without legitimate issue, to the throne.

Oldham, unfortunately, was destined to suffer the fate of satirists who base their major work on the topical, the event of the day. Once the events that occasioned the invective and abuse have faded from men's memories, the satires, which require extensive annotation to be understandable to later generations, are likely to remain unread. The subject of this study, however, was more than a fiery anti-Catholic, anti-Jesuit propagandist. As several chapters are intended to demonstrate, he was one of the first practitioners of the "imitation" of other writers—Juvenal, Horace, and Boileau, in particular. This trick of doing more than translating Horace, say, line by line or paraphrasing his sense, but actually changing the context to a contemporary one and alluding to figures and incidents of the time, reached a peak of perfection with Alexander Pope in the next century.

Most modern readers of Oldham also find his rugged spirit of independence refreshing and admirable. He was forced by circumstance to spend part of his career as an assistant schoolmaster in a remote village. Encouraged by some recognition from the fashionable Court Wits—Rochester, Sedley, Buckhurst—he attempted to lead an independent literary life in London, but met only hardship. Unlike many other young men of talent not smiled upon by fortune, he resisted the schoolmaster's or domestic chaplain's calling because he was too proud to sacrifice his independence and integrity for a modicum of security. In fact, he appears at his best and most endearing as a poet when he is proclaiming his independence and self-reliance.

Like those of other writers of his time, Oldham's works present textual problems and questions of attribution. Unfortunately for his reputation, there is no modern edition of his works. The only edition easily available to students is the 1854 edition of Robert Bell (reissued as a Centaur Classic in 1960 by the Southern Illinois University Press). Bell's edition omits nineteen of the works included in Edward Thompson's 1770 edition of the collected works, works considered likely to offend Victorian sensibilities. We can only hope that the long-promised edition of Harold F. Brooks, which he prepared as an Oxford D.Phil. dissertation in 1940, will eventually appear.

Fortunately for modern scholarship, however, Professor Elias Mengel, editor of Volume II of the Yale University Press *Poems on*

Affairs of State (*POAS*), includes in his edition a fully annotated and improved text of the *Satires Upon the Jesuits*. *POAS* was one of the collections of, among other things, Whig and anti-Catholic poems that became generally available after the Glorious Revolution. Professor Mengel's inclusion of the attack on the Jesuits, along with Dryden's *Absalom and Achitophel,* allows the reader to place Oldham's satire in the context of the political and religious satire of his time. The appearance of the Yale *POAS* II in 1965 has helped further the revaluation of Oldham prompted earlier by the patient and dedicated efforts of Harold F. Brooks to reestablish the reputation of an undeservedly forgotten poet.

My indebtedness to the labors of Professor Brooks will be apparent throughout this book. It would be ungrateful—and ungracious—of me not to make a special acknowledgment. I am also grateful to have had access to the collections of the Newberry Library and the libraries of Northwestern University and the University of Chicago.

One final word: as will become immediately apparent, this study is aimed at the nonspecialist reader. I have, therefore, followed modern spelling practice in quoting from Oldham and other writers of the time, except when it seemed that retaining original spelling was advisable. In addition, to make the text as self-contained as I could without any sacrifice of scholarly responsibility, I have tried to keep the amount of material relegated to notes to a minimum.

James Zigerell

Chronology

1653   John Oldham born August 9 at Shipton-Moyne in Gloucester, son and grandson of dissenting ministers.

1662   Father, ejected from rectorship, keeps a small school, where poet studies under his tutelage.

1668   At about this time, poet is sent to grammar school at Tetbury to prepare for university studies.

1670   Matriculates at St. Edmund's College, Oxford.

1671   Takes B.A. and returns home, probably to teach in father's school.

1674–1675   Writes some occasional verse and well-known panegyric on death of close friend, Charles Morwent.

1676   Becomes usher at John Shepheard's school in Croydon; composes some verse dedicated to local gentry; writes *Satire Against Virtue* which circulated in manuscript and probably occasioned visit to school of John Wilmot, Earl of Rochester, and fellow wits.

1677   As sequel to visit by Court Wits, and to cultivate relationship, Oldham writes some obscene verses (later printed in an Antwerp edition of Rochester's works) and a *Dithyrambic on Drinking*; has hopes of winning official notice at the Court through "Cosmelia," a lady-in-waiting in the household of the Duke of York, who places his ode on her marriage to William of Orange in hands of Princess Mary.

1678   Marriage ode printed by Herringman through good offices of Cosmelia, to whom he had also written several love poems; composes ode on Ben Jonson for projected edition of his works by Herringman.

1679   On September 6, Titus Oates appears before London magistrate Sir Edmund Berry Godfrey with details of alleged Popish Plot; several weeks later, the body of Godfrey is found in a ditch near Hampstead, run through by his own sword, after magistrate had disappeared several days earlier. Writes *Garnet's Ghost*, first of the *Satires Upon the*

Jesuits, occasioned by Oates's electrifying allegations of the plot against the king's life; satire published piratically; the *Satire Against Virtue* published by Herringman, who becomes Oldham's regular publisher.

1680 Leaves to try independent life in London where, according to "An Allusion to Martial," he lives in a garret "at the far end of Clerkenwell."

1681 Authorized edition of *Satires Upon the Jesuits*; *Some New Pieces*, including his imitation of Horace's *Ars Poetica*.

1682 Despite enough reader demand to warrant a second edition of *Satires Upon the Jesuits*, Oldham becomes a tutor again, this time to eldest son of Sir William Hickes of Rookwood in Essex; is thought to have made an abortive start on a study of medicine; declines to accompany family's son on Continental tour; after, perhaps, one more fling at an independent literary life in London, moves to Holme Pierrepoint in Nottinghamshire, where William Pierrepoint, fourth Earl of Kingston, is his patron.

1683 On December 7, dies of smallpox, his death cutting short a productive period of his career which began in 1681, with his best imitations of Roman poets and Boileau.

1684 Dryden's tribute, "To the Memory of Mr. Oldham," published in *The Remains of Mr. John Oldham*.

Chapter One

From Humble
Schoolmaster to Wit

The spirits of some poets are doomed to haunt the edges of the shades wherein dwell the ghosts of their more fortunate brothers whose literary reputations have outlived their own age. Later generations of readers either ignore these unlucky ones or, if they remember them at all, are unsure as to the lasting worth of their achievement. The dealers in literary reputations—the academic critics and literary historians—differ among themselves as to whether these unhappy spirits deserve standing as poets in themselves or are fit only to be regarded as figures foreshadowing or reflecting the qualities of their greater contemporaries.

So it is with the subject of this study, the Restoration satirist John Oldham. Although assured a pittance of immortality in a eulogy by John Dryden as one whose soul was "cast in the same poetick mould as mine," he is read today only by specialists in his age. The anthologies pay him scant attention. The older *Oxford Book of English Verse*, edited by Sir Arthur Quiller-Couch, for example, contains only ten lines from an elegy on a friend written when Oldham was just twenty-two; the new Oxford anthology edited by Helen Gardner contains no work of his at all. If he is remembered, he is remembered by students as the author of a fierce attack on the Jesuits and the Roman Catholic Church occasioned by the now-forgotten Popish Plot of his own time.

But the hasty judgment of George Saintsbury in his *History of English Poetry* that Oldham's fame is due only to "his period, his early death, and the magnificent eulogy of Dryden," although typical of later estimates, is unduly harsh, as, it is hoped, this study will demonstrate. Indeed, as this study will show, today's literary historians see in Oldham an important forerunner in the art of the imitation and topical satire, and accord him a rank as a satirist of the Restoration just below John Dryden, Samuel Butler, and Andrew Marvell.

Readers in his own time found such bite in his satire that they dubbed him an English Juvenal. Bonamy Dobrée in a prefatory essay to a 1960 reprint of Robert Bell's nineteenth-century edition of Oldham's works—still the only readily available edition—makes a case for keeping his memory alive:

> It is time that he was made more available, for though his importance may lie in the fact that his originality in satire paved the way for poets greater than he, he is worth reading for himself, for his energy, his use of language, and the strangeness of his flavour.[1]

Although he was born under unfriendly stars as the circumstances of his life made clear, he was befriended or, to put it more precisely, patronized by the Court Wits, the Earl of Rochester, Sir Charles Sedley, and the Earl of Dorset. They were gentlemen and noblemen who moved in the Court scene, had access to the king, and, more important for someone like Oldham aspiring to a career as poet and satirist, helped establish the fashionable literary taste. The net result of their patronage, such as it was, was that he managed to trade the penury and dreariness of a rural schoolmaster's life for a brief fling at the bitterness and disappointment of a Grub Street existence in London, where, in the spiteful words of Anthony Wood, a contemporary Oxford antiquary and biographer of Oxford-educated writers, he went to "set himself up for a wit."[2]

Oldham himself, echoing Milton's sentiments on the poet's lot in *Lycidas*, described his fate in resigned tones in a verse epistle called *Letter from the Country to a Friend in Town*:

> Poets are cullies, whom rook fame draws in
> And wheedles with deluding hopes to win.

Dead at the age of thirty, during the six years before his death, he completed the works—most written to specific occasions—that won him the acclaim of his own generation of writers and the respect of immediately succeeding ones. Untypically, since he was never fortune's darling, his major work, the vituperative *Satires Upon the Jesuits*, was prompted by an occasion that inflamed the entire nation and appeared at the very moment when Englishmen of all social classes were being carried away by an anti-Catholic, anti-papist, anti-Jesuit frenzy and were thus receptive to his potent and fiery propaganda. His expression of the right-thinking Englishman's loathing of Rome and her minions gained him a *succès d'estime*, if not success in the usual worldly sense.

A Short View of his Life and Career: "This vile and Wicked lust of poetry"

The details of Oldham's life are short in the telling. Those that have come down to later generations are set forth, more or less accurately, in an anonymous *Memoirs of the Life and Writings of Mr. John Oldham* that preceded the 1722 edition of the poet's works. The same memoir was later made the introductory part of a three-volume edition of the works edited in 1770 by one Edward Thompson, an eccentric sea captain and literary adventurer. Other details, scarce though they are, can be gathered from two manuscripts in Oldham's own hand in the Bodleian Library at Oxford.[3]

A minister's son, Oldham was born on August 9, 1653, at Shipton-Moyne, near Tetbury in Gloucester, where his grandfather also served as a minister. H. F. Brooks, who is the modern authority on Oldham, reports that local parish records contain the following entry regarding the poet's birth:

John Ouldham the sonne of John Ouldham the sonne of John Ouldham the elder minister was born August 9 and baptized August 18, 1653.[4]

The poet must have grown up in modest, or mean, circumstances. As is well known, the life of an ordinary clergyman and his family in the seventeenth century was difficult under any conditions. Indeed, in one of his earlier and better efforts in the Juvenalian vein, the *Satire Addressed to a Friend About to Leave the University,* Oldham set down for posterity the meannesses and indignities of the clerical life, a life often dependent on the favor of the great, with only a faint hope of "some slender benefice,"

> With this proviso bound, that he must wed
> My lady's antiquated waiting maid.

By his own admission, Macaulay took this picture as the model for his well-known sketch of a domestic chaplain in the opening volume of his *History of England.* Indeed, Oldham's childhood could not have been other than difficult, particularly since his father was a nonconformist minister who was ejected from a parish in Wiltshire while the poet was a boy.

One is tempted to conjecture, as surely some of his contemporaries did, that Oldham grew up harboring bitter feelings toward his father. The year after his death there was published in his *Remains* (1684) a scurrilous prose piece entitled *Character of a Certain Ugly old P—*, a nasty parody of the Theophrastan characters in vogue in the seventeenth century, appearing under names such as "Character of a Town-Gallant" or "Character of a Town Miss." Oldham's parson is described in revolting physical detail and is presented as a disgusting hypocrite. It is tempting to conclude that Oldham's growing up in a clerical household inspired this unpleasant portrait.

What is significant for the student, however, is that even though living in the home of a dissenting minister could have brought little in a material way, the experience must certainly have readied the poet for his career as an anti-Catholic polemicist and Protestant champion. Brooks notes in an invaluable essay on Oldham's poetry that

Oldham's horror of Catholic militancy and Catholic superstitions and corruptions may have first been implanted by his upbringing in his Presbyterian father's house.[5]

Much of the poet's early education, in addition to the anti-papist indoctrination noted by Brooks, was received at home. The details are recounted in the anonymous memoir mentioned above:

He was educated in Grammar-Learning under the care of his Father, till he was almost fit for the University; and to be completely qualified for that Purpose, he was sent to Tedbury-School [sic], where he spent about two years under the tuition of Mr. Henry Heaven, occasioned by the earnest Request of Alderman Yeat of Bristol, who having a Son at the same school, was desirous that Mr. Oldham should be his Companion, which would, as he thought, very much conduce to the Advancement of his Learning. This, for some time, retarded Mr. Oldham in the Prosecution of his own Studies; but for the Time he lost, in forwarding Mr. Yeat's Son, his Father afterwards made ample Amends.

This episode in the poet's early life is typical, in that for most of his life, except for a brief fling at independence in London, he was forced to accommodate himself to the wishes of the influential, frequently the fate, as he himself was to point out in the *Satire Addressed to a Friend*, as well as in other works, of both the clergyman and the poet. In 1670 he was sent to St. Edmund's Hall, Oxford, where he came to be regarded as a good Latinist, and, according to the waspish Anthony Wood, was observed "chiefly to addict himself to poetry."[6] He left the university in 1674, after taking the B.A., and returned home to live with his father.

Some Early Efforts at Verse

At about this time he wrote several poems which Brooks describes as "occasional pieces likely to recommend him to families of standing in the neighborhood."[7] Such was the lot of the impoverished writer of the late seventeenth century, forced to seek out the favor, pecuniary and otherwise, of the influential, while, ironically, as Alexander Beljame indicates in his classic study, *Men of Letters and the English Public in the Eighteenth Century*,

the author's custom of begging and accepting alms in return for obligatory flattery . . . was bound to lessen still further the scanty respect in which he was held.[8]

In 1675, a year after Oldham had returned home from the university to live with his father, a sad occurrence occasioned the first of his poems traceable with any assurance to a definite date. Charles Morwent, a young clergyman who was his close friend, died of the smallpox. His death prompted *To the Memory of Mr. Charles Morwent*, a panegyrical ode of forty-two stanzas that, besides being a respectable example of a form then much in vogue, contains several sincere and genuinely moving passages. (Indeed, the young Alexander Pope was to consider it one of Oldham's better pieces.) The anonymous *Memoirs of His Life and Writings* informs us that

the Loss of the hopeful young Gentleman, and being separated from the rest of his University Friends, made a Home-restraint sit very heavy upon Mr. Oldham.

The lament for Morwent is a panegyric on his young friend and suffers from all the rhetorical excesses of that form. It is, however, a skillful adaptation of the pastoral elegy, the conventions of which go back to Theocritus, Bion, and Moschus and found memorable expression for the generation preceding Oldham's in Milton's *Lycidas* (1637): mythological figures; nature presented in the guise of a mourner; reflections on the inscrutability of the divine will; the acceptance of death as the gateway to eternal life and fame; the climactic ascent of the dead one to the heavens to take his or her place among the constellations. Oldham's fifteen-line stanzas have the solemnity and rhetorical elaboration suitable to the occasion. The rhyme scheme has the complexity associated with the ode, rhyming couplets giving way at some point in every stanza to triplets and alternating rhymes.

Oldham, too, shifts refreshingly from the artificialities of the pastoral elegy, with "all Helicon" paying its "tribute" to the departed one, and the fulsome praise of the panegyric, which attributes a truly heroic combination of virtues to the deceased, to expressions of genuine feeling—

> So gentle was thy pilgrimage beneath,
> Time's unheard feet scarce make less noise.

He also effects the change of mood from grief to resignation and near-exaltation, conventional in the elegy, with notable skill. He makes use of conceits worthy of Cowley. As a compass needle points north (a metaphysical image he was fond of), as a flame rises upward, or as a prisoner longs for freedom, Morwent's spirit was

> . . . vexed and chafed, and still desired to be,
> Released to the sweet freedom of eternity.

Finally, as the convention dictated, there is the inevitable apotheosis, with the departed one's soul climbing to the "joyful sky," and shining among the stars, his memory living on to light others' way.

To the Memory of Mr. Charles Morwent, a sustained effort in a demanding form, must have marked Oldham in local circles as a young man who was possessed of real poetic gifts. Though labored and repetitious, the elegy displays an inventiveness and verbal facility remarkable in a poet of only twenty-two years. Robert Bell compares it to Dryden's panegyrical verses on Lord Hastings, composed when Dryden was only seventeen. Overlooking the disparity in the ages of the poets, Bell finds Oldham's conceits more dignified and appropriate to the occasion.[9]

Whether Morwent's death was a determining factor or not, shortly afterwards Oldham left home to accept the lowly position of usher in a charity school at Croydon in Surrey. In all likelihood, conditions at home must have been far from tolerable. Brooks conjectures that the poem commemorating Morwent may have helped Oldham escape, since the headmaster whose assistant he became, one John Shepheard, was a relative of the deceased. But required to subsist on what the memoirist calls a "mean Salary" and perform the lowliest of academic chores, he surely must have bridled under his new living conditions, conditions that inspired these bitter reflections in his *Satire to a Friend About to Leave the University*:

> Where you, for recompense of all your pains,
> Shall hardly reach a common fiddler's pain.

To exacerbate his feeling of unhappiness and discontent, he may also have felt romantic urgings at about the time he moved to Croydon. Several poems written about 1671—"Some Verses on Presenting a Book to Cosmelia," "The Parting," "Complaining of Absence," and "Promising a Visit"—hint at an attachment that went much beyond what in that age was enough to occasion poetical exercises. For that matter, these verses are the only love poems to be found in Oldham's works. Bell, the editor of the bowdlerized 1854 edition of the poems who seemingly felt compelled to look for opportunities to apologize for the poet's indelicacy and crudeness, concedes that even though Oldham's strength never lay in "pathos or tenderness," there is "much feeling and delicacy in these little pieces."[10]

"On Presenting a Book to Cosmelia" is, on the whole, a conventional exercise organized around several conceits in a vaguely metaphysical fashion. It seems thoroughly artificial to a modern reader. It is addressed to a young lady who was a hairdresser to the Duke of York's daughter Mary. Oldham, it seems, clung to the hope for a time that he might gain some notice at Court. Brooks cites a Latin letter in which the poet "refers to a lady who is a coiffeuse, and perhaps, he adds slyly, has charge of her rouge too."[11]

The lines to Cosmelia show Oldham to have been an able student and imitator of the poets of his time, as the opening command, with

its definite echo of Edmund Waller's "Go, Lovely Rose," demonstrates:

> Go, humble gift, go to that matchless saint,
> Of who thou only wast a copy meant;
> And all that's read in thee, more richly find
> Comprised in the fair volume of her mind.

The rest of the poem strings together a series of extravagant tributes
to the goodness and innocence of the young lady addressed, whether
she was real, imaginary, or something in between. Oldham struggles
bravely to yoke together these heterogeneous notions in the manner
Samuel Johnson was to describe in the next century in his *Life of
Cowley* as the "metaphysical." But his efforts met with only modest
success, as the following lines describing the natural beauty of
Cosmelia and the joy she finds in practising goodness and other
virtues for their own sakes show:

> The scattered glories of her happy sex
> In her bright soul as in their centre mix:
> And all that they possess but by retail,
> She hers by just monopoly can call.

Such immature flings at metaphysical conceits, with their echoes of
Donne and Cowley, were not as his later development makes clear,
in a vein congenial to Oldham's temperament and inclinations. But
it should be noted in passing that the above lines show Oldham
developing his figures and thought couplet by couplet, rather than
over longer stretches—a forecast of what was to be done in the next
century with elegance and polish by a poet of Pope's talent.

All in all, this early attempt at love poetry shows Oldham to have
been a young poet of some talent, his lines and figures, imitative
though they are, disclosing signs of real inventiveness. It is also
interesting to note that Oldham liked to practice an economy common to poets of all ages. As Robert Bell notes, some of the lines
dedicated to Cosmelia were appropriated from the ode on the memory
of Morwent, which had not as yet been published. For example, of
Cosmelia's virtues, he writes:

> Her virtue scorns at a low pitch to fly,
> 'Tis all free choice, nought of necessity;

Of the dead Morwent's virtue, he says:

> Thine a far nobler pitch did fly,
> 'Twas all free choice, nought of necessity.

What counts is that the lines apply in both instances.

In the other two early love poems, Oldham plays the lover separated from the object of his love. In the "Parting" he laments his
absence from his loved one by tying together several long similes
in an artificial Miltonic manner, one of which likens the lovers'
parting to a young merchant's sailing off on a long voyage, looking
back longingly at the land as it fades slowly from sight:

> And when at length the launching vessel flies,
> And severs first his lips, and then his eyes,
> Long he looks back to see what he adores,
> And, while he may, views the belovèd shores.

"Complaining of Absence," however, is much less artificial and hints
at a stronger feeling and a real attachment to a flesh-and-blood lady.
The opening lines have the directness that bespeaks a felt emotion:

> Ten days (if I forget not) wasted are
> (A year in any lover's calendar)
> Since I was forced to part, and bid adieu
> To all my joy and happiness in you.

Even lines like the following, despite the conventional and labored
likening of the lover's position to that of the Christian deprived of
the vision of divine glory while he still struggles on earth as part of
the Church Militant, have an authenticity. They come from a poet
whose lot in life was never easy:

> But I, poor lover militant below,
> The cares and troubles of full life must know;
> Must toil for that which does on others wait,
> And undergo the drudgery of fate.

His love, whether real or not, occasioned passable poetic efforts. The
lines just quoted, as well as others in his early and few attempts at
love poems, are touching in that they suggest the general wretched-

ness and emptiness of the poet's life as a lowly schoolmaster, rather
than the misery of the disappointed lover.

As these early efforts make clear, Oldham did aspire to write, and
could do so creditably, in a softer vein than his best-known works
would suggest. But, on the whole, his voice in love verses is an
unconvincing one. These poems are little more than moderately
interesting exercises in the love conventions of earlier generations.
Yet they do reveal a young poet who had read widely and eagerly
in the classics and the English writers of the seventeenth and earlier
centuries. "Promising a Visit," for example, a poem of thirty-two
lines bewailing his separation from Cosmelia, is a pastiche of images
from the Elizabethan sonneteers and an inventory of pseudo-meta-
physical conceits elaborated and developed over quatrains composed
of rhyming couplets:

> Sooner may art, and easier for, divide
> The soft embracing waters of the tide,
> Which with united friendship still rejoin,
> Than part my eyes, my arms, or lips from thine . . .
>
> Not the touched needle (emblem of my soul)
> With greater reverence trembles to its pole,
> Nor flames with surer instinct upwards go,
> Than mine, and all their motives, tend to you.

A study of these early, untypical poems of Oldham is rewarding in
that it affords glimpses into the life of a talented young man struggling to make his way as a poet. An important part of the struggle
was to find a patron or protector, a task at which he was only moderately successful, his success being limited to finding places as tutor
or companion in the homes of the wealthy. In 1677, for example,
while he was at Croydon, he wrote in great haste a creditable Pindaric ode on the marriage of William and Mary which he hoped
would bring him to the attention of influential people at Court. The
work did not achieve its purpose, although, as we shall see later,
it opened other doors. The ode did reach the Court through the good
offices of the Cosmelia already mentioned. But as Brooks reports in
his *Bibliography*, the manuscript collection of Oldham's works in
the Bodleian contains a draft of a Latin letter in which the poet
notes sadly that, despite the ode's coming to the attention of the

royal bride ("Herae"), he knew only that he had wasted both midnight oil and effort.

From its very beginning, Oldham's career seems a model of the Grub Street writer's life that was to become so familiar in the next century. We remember how Samuel Johnson bristled under the necessity of currying the favor of the rich and the influential. No opportunity to dedicate a poem to someone who might become a protector and patron could be lost.

Some of Oldham's earliest works were dedicated to prominent families near Shipton-Moyne. "To Madam L. E. Upon Her Recovery from a Late Sickness" is a panegyric in celebration of the return to health of a lady in the neighborhood. Brooks conjectures that the lady was one Lady Estcourt of a nearby estate.[12] This effort and "On the Death of Mrs. Katharine Kingscote," a poem memorializing the eleven-year-old daughter of another influential family, must both be classified as juvenilia. Like the love poems, both are filled with echoes of other poets, especially Cowley and Waller, both contain strained conceits and exaggerations of the metaphysical kind, both draw upon the conventions of the pastoral elegy popular at the time. The dead child is a saint who, like a star, is seen to

> mount the sky
> And with new whiteness paint the galaxy.

So pure and noble was she in life that

> By her we credit what the learnèd tell
> That many angels on one point can dwell.

The more fortunate Madame L. E. is both the subject of the panegyric and the muse invoked by the poet. Heaven desired her to fill an "empty seat," but at last growing

> conscious that its power
> Could scarce what was to die with you restore,

decided to spare such glory for this world's sake and delay her apotheosis. Catching some of the grace of a Cavalier poet—except for the inelegant "snatched"—Oldham assures the lady that her beauty has not been impaired, for

That sun shall with interest repay
All the lost beauty sickness snatched away.

Oldham must have been busy at Croydon. In fact, Brooks in the *Bibliography* reports that a part of the Bodleian manuscript in Oldham's autograph

consists of what were originally loose leaves or groups of leaves; many of Oldham's verses were scribbled on the back of margins of his pupils' school exercises.[13]

While there, Oldham also wrote an elegy on the death of Harmon Atwood (d. 1677), whose niece the headmaster of his school had married. The memorial is a Pindaric ode, a form that, as will be indicated later, the poet employed a number of times. Atwood, who was a lawyer, is presented as a glory to the law in a corrupt age, a paragon of generosity, a man whose religion was powerful enough to counteract lewd poets and the stage,

And proselyte as fast as they debauch the stage.

From his study of the Bodleian manuscript, Brooks also concludes that Oldham wrote two paraphrases of Scripture for the family of Sir Nicholas Carew of Beddington, with whom he spent Christmas in 1676.[14] Both are written in a loose Pindaric form. One, a paraphrase of the 137th Psalm, although of little interest as a composition in its own right, does forecast some of the topical concerns that later on were to gain the poet a reputation. Lines like the following, for example, suggest his preoccupation with the threat of popery, a concern that was to receive such fiery expression in the *Satires Upon the Jesuits*:

Oh, sacred temple, once the Almighty's
blessed abode,
Now quite forsaken by our angry God:

Like many of his contemporaries, whose fears and fury he was to voice, Oldham recognized the threat posed by those who were plotting against king and country and recalled the allegations that Catholics had set the Great Fire of 1666 which had destroyed four-fifths of London—

> Who laughed to see our flaming city burn,
> And wished it might to ashes turn.

Oldham must have remained preoccupied with the Catholic threat throughout his life. The Bodleian manuscript collection shows that while at the school in Croydon he assigned his pupils Latin verses on themes such as the Gunpowder Plot.

That Oldham possessed a sure instinct for what alarmed the true blue Protestant breast is suggested by the other scriptural paraphrase of his Croydon days, "David's Lamentations for the Death of Saul and Jonathan." As students of the period are well aware, paraphrasing and retelling biblical narratives for the sake of indicating parallels to contemporary events and persons was a favorite practice. Biblical accounts of David and incidents from his life were employed to reflect on Charles II and the current political situation: Dryden was to use the biblical parallels of David and his sons to brilliant effect in *Absalom and Achitophel*, which appeared several years later, in 1689. Oldham, in his rather pedestrian effort, expands David's lament for Saul and his son Jonathan killed at the hands of the Philistines, as contained in the Second Book of Kings. Oldham surely intended his readers to associate Israel's sad plight after the death of Saul and Jonathan with the plight of an England threatened by the return of popery and the political chicanery of Catholic France—

> Ah, wretched Israel! ah, unhappy state!
> Exposed to all the bolts of angry fate!

If, indeed, Oldham composed the paraphrase for the Carew household, his audience must have been struck by the similarities to the state of affairs in the kingdom, what with the country torn by rivalries between Cavalier and Puritan, the growing factionalism of the Country and the Town, and the Romish threat.

Needless to say, poems of this kind hold only slight interest in themselves, and are not of the quality the lover of poetry expects from a favorite anthology. They are the kinds of exercises a struggling poet hoped would gain him the attention of people who might further his career. They do command the attention of the literary historian in that they must have signaled to some contemporaries the appearance of a young man of talent. In addition, despite their artificiality and derivative qualities, they afford affecting glimpses into the harshness of the youthful Oldham's life, as when, as an aspirant to literary reputation and prosperity, he describes himself in "Complaining of Absence" as one who

> Must toil for that which does on others wait,
> And undergo the drudgery of fate.

If nothing else, lines as well turned and apt as these endear their author to a modern reader. Many deserving young men—and young women—of all ages have had to "toil for that which does on others wait."

The Attention of the Wits

His lowliness of station aside, Oldham's early works did circulate in manuscript and came to the attention of some of the Court Wits. The memoirs record what must have been a memorable event in his life at Croydon when

... he received a Visit from the Earl of Rochester, the Earl of Dorset, Sir Charles Sedley, and other Persons of Distinction, merely upon the reputation of some of his Verses, which they had seen in Manuscript.

One of the verses that commended him to their attention was *A Satire Against Virtue*, a seemingly blasphemous, but actually ironic, Pindaric which later appeared in a collection of Rochester's poems printed in Antwerp in 1680. The satire was certainly one that would have caught the eye of Rochester. As a matter of fact, the long title of the manuscript copy alludes to one of the earl's more notorious exploits: *Supposed to be Spoken by a Court Hector at the Breaking of the Dial in Privy Garden*. Although the printed editions of the satire do not mention the episode of the sundial, Brooks reports that Oldham's autograph fair copy in the Bodleian does give it as the occasion. Rochester's biographers record that on June 25, 1675, he and several other of the Court Wits broke into the Privy Garden at

Whitehall after a night of carousing. There they came upon the king's sundial, an arrangement of glass spheres in the shape of a phallus. Rochester shouted an obscene imprecation, and, as his most recent editor, David Vieth, puts it, the next moment "he had demolished the offending instrument."[15]

Oldham's having succeeded in attracting the attention of the notorious wits sparked the following comment from Anthony Wood, which the poet's memoirist took as an "opprobrious attack":

...he became acquainted with that noted poet for obscenity, and blasphemy, John earl of Rochester, who seemed delighted in the mad ranting, and debauched specimens of poetry of this author Oldham.[16]

The memoirs relate an amusing and touching anecdote concerning the Croydon visit that made the rounds of the coffeehouses and found its way into biographical dictionaries. The headmaster at Croydon, fancying that the distinguished and brilliant visitors had come to see him, turned himself out in what little finery he could muster and went out to receive his guests. "When the tottering Pedagogue made his entry," the memoirs report, "they were all on the Laugh." Once he was informed that the company had come to meet his talented usher, the harmless old man confessed with disarming candor that "he had not Wit or Learning enough for such good Company."

Edward Thompson, Oldham's first editor, notes that the poet's

first Introduction to the salacious Wits of that Wanton age...brought him acquainted with some other Persons of Distinction, who afterward proved his most steady Friends and Patrons.

The memoirs also indicate that "this Adventure was of some Length, and brought him to the Acquaintance of some other Persons of Note." This recognition of his talent by such prominent figures probably led at the end of his third year at Croydon to his being recommended by Harman Atwood, a Surrey lawyer, to Sir Edmund Thurland, a judge in the same county, as tutor to his two grandsons. What the "Adventure" meant to his advancement as a poet is a matter open to question. He probably had the favor of the Court Wits in mind when he wrote several obscene satires and an erotic poem called "The Dream" about the Cosmelia we have already met. The satires include *Upon the Author of the Play Called Sodom, Sardanapalus*, and a

Dithyrambic on Drinking. The first two, as Brooks indicates in the *Bibliography*, were intended to remain in manuscript. As already indicated, some of Oldham's poems, including the salacious *Upon the Author of a Play Called Sodom*, were printed in an Antwerp collection of Rochester's works, a collection considered so scandalous that the *London Gazette* advertised a reward of five pounds to anyone who could help the authorities "discover" the whereabouts of the printers.

It seems likely, however, as the memoirs state, that one outcome of the Croydon visit was that when Oldham went to London, his "Croyden-Visiters [*sic*] . . . brought Him acquainted with Mr. Dryden." These aristocratic wits delighted in discovering needy and talented young men, especially ones who seemingly shared their own flair for both the acidulous and the scandalous. In his study of the Restoration poet Charles Sedley published in 1927, V. De Sola Pinto notes how Sedley and the other wits liked to take fledgling poets under their wing—including, by the way, the young Matthew Prior. In any event, whatever favor he earned with Rochester and the circle of wits must certainly have opened literary groups to Oldham when he went to London in 1681. More censorious contemporary observers, of course, must have shared Anthony Wood's view that Oldham and the licentious Rochester were birds of a feather, kindred spirits attracted to each other by a common love of vice.

All in all, there are no indications that the Croydon visit brought any noticeable and immediate improvement in the poet's way of life, at least during the year it took place. Oldham remained in Croydon for about another three years. A reader can gather his feelings about his life there as a schoolmaster's assistant from the already cited and forceful *Satire Addressed to a Friend That Is About to Leave the University*. In this highly readable poem, which stands in the line of didactic verse that reached an apex in Pope's *Moral Epistles*, the poet ticks off for a friend, a fellow spirit who also has been shunned by Lady Fortune, the prospects for anyone who turns schoolmaster. The fact is that the job is seldom a first choice, but a second or third one, something taken on when all else fails:

> For want of better opportunity,
> A school must your next sanctuary be.
> Go, wed some grammar-bridewell, and a wife,
> And there beat Greek and Latin for your life.

The rewards for beating Latin and Greek are meager indeed:

> For when you've toiled, and laboured all you can,
> To dung and cultivate a barren brain,
> A dancing master shall be better paid,
> Though he instructs the heels, and you the head.

While he remained at Croydon, nonetheless, Oldham bravely continued to seek recognition at the Court and elsewhere. As we have seen, he hoped that the verses he had written to commemorate the marriage of William and Mary in 1677 would gain him official attention. As it happened, they were the first of his works to find their way into print. The same Cosmelia to whom he had addressed love verses and who introduced the commemorative ode on the royal marriage to the Court managed to get it to the printer Herringman.

Thus, the episode of the ode on the marriage of William and Mary opened another avenue of opportunity. The ode's finding its way to Herringman acquainted him with the same printer's plan to publish an edition of the works of Ben Jonson, a poet with whom he felt a natural affinity and with whom he shared a strong desire to castigate the vices of mankind. In 1678, in fact, Oldham composed an ode entitled *Upon the Works of Ben Jonson*, a creditable effort to be discussed in detail later in this study. Brooks's conclusion is that he wrote the ode "in the hope of seeing it prefixed to the new edition."[17] In what was to become a tradition of later Grub Street writers, he took his subjects wherever he could find them.

The ode on the royal wedding, *Upon the Marriage of the Prince of Orange with the Lady Mary*, is worthy of further attention in connection with its author's ambitions as a writer. Besides standing as a respectable example of the then-popular panegyric form, it is informed by a shrewd sense of what was politic on the part of someone seeking official favor during the period of the Glorious Revolution. In fact, the theme is that of Oldham's principal work, *The Satires Upon the Jesuits*. The first of the ode's five stanzas contains the fulsome praise of royalty that was conventional, and prudent, at the time:

> As when of old, some bright and heavenly dame
> A god of equal majesty did wed;

> Straight through the court above the tidings spread,
> Straight at the news the immortal offspring came,
> And all the deities did the high nuptials grace.

But once the amenities have been got out of the way, the second and third stanzas cleverly hail the union as one cementing a league between the Protestant powers that halted the advance of France and Catholicism. The match is a glorious tribute to the Glorious Revolution:

> This union by no blood cemented is,
> Nor did its harmony from jars and discord rise.

It is the last stanza, however, with its touch of inadvertent irony, that most catches the attention of a modern reader. The poet calls for a fruitful union in one that was to be without issue:

> May you be fruitful in as numerous store
> Of princely births, as she who your great father bore.

To conclude this consideration of the young poet's attempts to better his lot while still at Croydon, we can say that his access to the Court through Cosmelia gained him little in any tangible sense. What slight bettering of his lot resulted can with greater justice be attributed to his having made the acquaintance of the local gentry, especially the already mentioned Harman Atwood, an uncle of the headmaster, and Sir Nicholas Carew. As we have seen, Atwood recommended the poet to the attention of Sir Edward Thurland, the judge in the Exchequer who was seeking a tutor for his grandson.

In any event, Oldham left Croydon for Reigate, where he took up his post as tutor. There he remained until 1681, when he moved to the household of Sir William Hicks to become tutor to his son. The memoirs report that it was while he was in the Hicks' household that, desperate to find a way to a decent livelihood and encouraged by a friend of his employer's, he made an abortive start on the study of medicine. He studied for a while with Richard Lower, a distinguished doctor referred to in his imitation of Horace's *Ars Poetica* as a fine physician, but not in the top rank. But, for all his leanings toward medicine, the memoirs tell us that

... the Bent of His Poetical Genius had too strong a Byas upon his inclination to become a Proficient in any School but that of the Muses.

The school of the Muses, of course, was to be found only in London.

The Call to London

It is not surprising that an aspiring and already productive young poet would be willing to leave the relative security of a well-to-do gentleman's household and venture on a literary career in London. In the *Letters from the Country to a Friend in Town*, written in 1678 while he was still resident at Reigate, Oldham rehearsed in an Horatian manner his reasons for serving poetry, which he dubs variously as the "worst of jilts, a muse," "trifling barren trade," "wild caprice," "heavy curse," "raving fit." In a long indecent simile, one certainly designed to catch the attention of the rakes whose goodwill he was courting, he complains:

> As a dry lecher pumped of all my store,
> I loathe the thing, cause I can do't no more:
> But, when I once begin to find again
> Recruits of matter in my pregnant brain,
> Again, more eager, I the hunt pursue,
> And with fresh vigour the loved sport renew:
> Tickled with some strange pleasure, which I find,
> And think a secrecy to all mankind,
> I please myself with vain, false delight,
> And count none happy, but the fops that write.

This verse epistle, its mock-seriousness only a fashionable veneer, strikes a responsive chord in a modern reader through its touching expressions of hope for success and recognition, the hope every gifted but poor young writer or artist harbors as he dreams of setting out for the metropolis to seek his fame and fortune. As the verse letter opens, the speaker likens himself in a long simile to the exiled Ovid devouring long-awaited letters from literary friends in far-off Rome—

> Such welcome here, dear sir, your letter had.

Rochester, we must also remember, had suffered banishment from the Court, when, in 1675, he had insulted the Duchess of Portsmouth, the king's mistress. Oldham was sure that his reference to Ovid's "Scythian exile" would find an echo in his admired Rochester's own experience.

As the poem continues, he modestly disclaims the praise heaped upon him by a gracious correspondent—Rochester again?—to whom praises "justlier all belong . . . who so well teach and practise wit." But his acknowledged limitation notwithstanding, the call to the poet's life is irresistible:

> Here or in town, at London or at Rome
> Rich or a beggar, free or in the Fleet,
> Whate'er my fate is, 'tis my fate to write.

It should be noted that Oldham always is interesting when he writes about the craft and the career of the writer. London beckoned, and he declined the invitation to accompany his pupil, the young Mr. Hicks, on the Grand Tour, even though, as the memoirs put it, he was "earnestly pressed to go abroad with Him." Instead, in the blunt words of the memoirist,

He took a grateful Leave of this Family, and with a small Sum of Money he had saved, hastened to London, and became a perfect Votary to the Bottle.

His reported addiction to wine must not have affected his charm of manner, for everyone who knew him, the memoirs continue, "acknowledged his Conversation was inexpressibly agreeable," so that he had not

. . . taken up his residence long in London before he was found out by his Croyden-Visiters. . . .

Throughout his stay in London he retained his devotion to Rochester, whom he always regarded as a mentor. He expressed this regard in a dedication to a translation of Bion's "Lamentation upon Adonis," and in a preface to a collection of his own verses he called him an "incomparable person, of whom nothing can be said, or thought, which his deserts do not surmount." Despite this warm tribute and the fact that, as the Bodleian manuscript collection shows, he copied out certain verses by Rochester, there is no real warrant for concluding that the relationship between the two poets was one of friendship, or even that between an aristocratic patron and a clever young poet. But there is no doubt that Rochester exerted a strong influence on his younger fellow-satirist. One of the most useful commentaries on Oldham's work is to be found in Rachel Trickett's valuable study of satire, *The Honest Muse* (1967). In a chapter called "Conventions of Satire," she notes:

His [Rochester's] strongest and most lasting influence was on Oldham, whose masculine and original genius was fascinated by his brilliant flexibility.[18]

In the aforementioned "Lamentation upon Adonis," intended as an elegy on the departed Rochester, Oldham acknowledged his debt:

> Others, thy flocks, thy lands, thy riches have,
> To me, thou didst thy pipe and skill vouchsafe.

As already noted, there is no evidence that his familiarity, if such it can be called, with the gifted rake brought him any advantage other than that of "pipe and skill." Johann Prinz, author of an older and outdated, but still valuable, study of Rochester, sums up the matter fairly, although he underestimates Oldham's talent as a writer, in the following statement:

Oldham certainly had wit enough and enough inclination to the obscene to please a character like Rochester, but there is nothing to show that his meeting with him [i.e., Rochester] had any direct effect upon his literary career.[19]

It is possible, however, that Rochester brought him to the attention of the Earl of Kingston who, as we shall see, took him under his protection when he left London.

In considering Oldham's attempt at a literary career in London, a reader must keep in mind that when the poet left the country for the town, and, in Anthony Wood's spiteful words, "set up for a wit," he had every reason to be confident of his own abilities. When he arrived, he already had a substantial body of work to his credit.

The autograph manuscript book in the Bodleian Library shows that he had completed the first book of the *Satires Upon the Jesuits*, his major work, early on. It had been printed, without his consent, as a broadside in 1679. In fact, by the time he departed for the capital in 1681, the entire series of four satires had been published, no mean feat for a poet still short of his thirtieth year.

His response to the pirated broadside of 1669 was entirely in character. When the text, an inaccurate one, was later reprinted by the printer Hindmarsh without correction in the first authorized edition of the *Satires*, he decided to strike back. The whole misadventure occasioned his awkwardly titled *Upon a Printer that exposed him by printing a piece of him grossly mangled and faulty*. This verse is interesting in that it reveals Oldham's strong sense of mission as a satirist, as well as his Juvenalian flair for abuse. Echoing famous lines in the first satire of Juvenal, he introduces himself as someone who is

> Born to chastise the vices of the age
> Which pulpits dare not, nor the very stage.

In another line he announces with an authoritative ring that

> Satire's my only province and delight—

a line which, inevitably, brings to mind the memorable description of Oldham's person as given in the memoirs of his life prefacing editions of his work, which we have cited several times thus far:

As to the Person of Mr. Oldham, Mr. Slater a Bookseller now at Eton, who served his Apprenticeship at Oxford, assured us he knew Him well, and was often happy in his Company. He said, his Stature was Tall, the Make of his Body very thin, his Face long, his Nose prominent, his Aspect unpromising, but Satire was in his Eye.

While still at Croydon, Oldham had also finished the *Satire Against Virtue*, a work which, as already noted, gained him some reputation among the literati through its having made the rounds of the coffee-houses in manuscript. This was his earliest attempt in the slashing satiric mode with which his name is linked by the literary historians.

On the whole, however, little is known about the final period of

Oldham's short life, a part of which he spent in London. Everyone must agree with Brooks that it is regrettable that there is so little information about Oldham's last period.

both because it was so fruitful and because if Dryden had any personal acquaintance with him it must have been at this time.[20]

It is reasonable to suppose on the basis of Dryden's noble and moving elegy that there may well have been some kind of personal relationship between him and the hapless Oldham. It seems likely that the great Dryden, one of whose most endearing qualities, as Macaulay once expressed it, was a "hearty and generous admiration for the talents of others," was well disposed toward him.

In any event, his brief career in London must have confirmed for him what he already had learned before his arrival: that is, the muse is a cruel mistress, often denying even the smallest comforts to those who follow her to the exclusion of all else. In his *Satire Dissuading from Poetry* he was to tick off for readers the woes and disappointments awaiting those who spend their lives in the service of the muse. The ghost of Edmund Spenser is made to complain:

> . . . grant thy poetry should find success,
> And, which is rare, the squeamish critics please:
>
> .   .   .
>
> If thou expectest aught but empty fame,
> Condemn thy hopes and labours to the flame,
> The rich have now learned only to admire.

Yet the satire concludes with a vision of Spenser's shade bearing a book "inscribed with Fairie Queen," and confessing that, despite all that has been said, the true poet cannot be dissuaded from his foolish course:

> Mayst thou go on unpitied, till thou be
> Brought to the parish . . . and beggary.

Oldham found another occasion to repeat this melancholy cry in an author's advertisement he wrote for an edition of his works which was published in 1684, shortly after his death. Complaining of being without a patron at the moment, he says caustically in this advertisement, that he has hopes of finding one in the future, when

he means to have ready a very Sparkish Dedication, if he can get himself
known to some Great Man, that will give a good parcel of Guineas for
being handsomely flattered.

Another work, written in imitation of the Roman poet Martial, "An
Allusion to Martial, Book 1, Epigram 118," affords further glimpses
into the circumstances of life in London without the help of a "Great
Man." The speaker in the poem is approached by a type familiar in
Roman satire, the leech. This one asks if he can send a boy to borrow
one of the poet's books of verse. Besides containing an authentic
biographic detail, the answer suggests the poverty and deprivation
Oldham had to endure while in London in search of fame and fortune:

> 'tis a long way to where I dwell,
> At farther end of Clerkenwell:
> There is a garret near the sky,
> Above five pairs of stairs I lie.

The imitation concludes, of course, with the poet-speaker suggesting
that if his parasitic acquaintance wants to do what is really the last
thing he has in mind, he can walk to a bookstall nearby where the
volume is on sale for a half crown. But he adds bitterly that he is
well aware that the would-be borrower would not give a half crown
for both the book and its author—a melancholy fact of life in Martial's
Rome as well as in Oldham's London.

The unlucky poet must have had many an occasion to curse his
"rhyming stars" while trying to work in his London garret. Since he
had achieved some renown, albeit one limited to a narrow circle of
admirers, and at least a *succès de scandale* from his obscene verses, he
must have come to the capital full of hope for a rewarding career and
life as a writer. But the London stay proved to be little more than a
bitter and continuing disappointment to him, as he reminds the reader
in his *Satire Dissuading from Poetry*:

> My own hard usage I need not press,
> Where you every day before you face
> Plenty of fresh resembling instances.

He says of Samuel Butler of *Hudibras* fame what the reader is meant
to apply to him and his own inglorious career in London:

> On Butler who can think without just rage,
> The glory and the scandal of the age?
> Fair stood his hopes, when first he came to town,
> Met everywhere with welcomes of renown . . .
> But what reward for all had he at last,
> After a life in dull expectance passed?
> The wretch at summing up his misspent days
> Found nothing left, but poverty and praise . . .

Indeed, the epitaph on Butler's monument of 1720 in Westminster gives voice to the kind of fate reserved for many poets in Oldham's age:

> While Butler, needy wretch, was yet alive
> No generous patron would a dinner give.
> See him when starv'd to death and turn'd to dust
> Presented with a monumental bust,
> The poet's fate is here an emblem show'n;
> He asked for bread and he received a stone.

These are lines worthy of Oldham himself. But the fact is—a theme Alexander Beljame develops in detail in *Men of Letters and the English Public in the Eighteenth Century*—there did not yet exist in Oldham's time a "public for literature," as the term is understood nowadays. Instead there were only narrow circles of readers whose patronage had to be sought by the writer:

Neither the word ["public"] nor the thing existed. The author saw before him only a coterie, too exclusive not to be all powerful, too powerful not to command obedience. . . . From the moment that a man adopted the career of a writer he was obliged to swear allegiance to a fashionable society and make himself a courtier—or die of hunger.[21]

In quest of recognition and patronage, Oldham probably played assiduously at being the wit. A talented paraphraser and imitator of the ancients, he translated the Latin poets—Ovid and Petronius, for example—whose salaciousness of theme was likely to appeal to the Wits. His "Fragment of Petronius Paraphras'd" is a typical instance. This is a complaint about the brief pleasures of physical love in the familiar *post coitrum tristis* vein—

> I hate fruition, now 'tis past,
> 'Tis all but nastiness at best.

This attitude toward the pleasures of love, one firmly established in the erotic poetry of Ovid, is also one, as Oldham well knew, that holds appeal for sated voluptuaries of all ages. Pleasure is not in the act itself, but in the anticipation of the act. Oldham renders Petronius's resigned lines as follows:

> Then let us not too eager run,
> By passion blindly hurried on.

In his *Bibliography* Brooks concludes, on the basis of strong internal evidence, that Oldham tried his hand at out-and-out pornographic verse in *"Sardanapalus"* and *"Upon the Author of the Play Call'd Sodom,"* efforts which must have delighted his well-wishers among the wits at Court. He never claimed authorship, however. Brooks notes:

It need cause no surprise that he never claimed *Sardanapalus*: it is pornographic, like the verses *Upon the Author of the Play Call'd Sodom*, which he likewise never referred to in print, but which may be seen in process of composition in his autograph MS. Doubtless he repented of both pieces.

Sardanapalus, according to Greek legend, was the last great king of Assyria who, while being besieged, burned himself and his wives to death in his palace.

It is unlikely that Oldham really enjoyed overmuch the pleasures of loose living, despite the addiction to the bottle with which he is credited by Anthony Wood and writers of later biographical sketches. In a prose meditation, published along with his *Remains*, in 1684, the year after his death, he asserts that he tried the "delights and pleasures of the world" and found them "empty." Even if the Bible and the divines did not teach men to despise them, he would have despised them anyway "by a greatness of soul," something a reader is inclined to believe of him, even though statements of contrition for misspent lives were often little more than conventions designed to placate preachers and divines. In addition, Oldham had before him as example the repentance of Rochester for a licentious life.

Last Days

In 1682 Oldham put himself under the protection of the Earl of Kingston in Nottinghamshire. We have already noted that his association with Rochester may have brought him to the attention of this nobleman. As the writer of the anonymous memoirs puts it:

... the Earl of Kingston continued his most sincere friend, and took Him solely under his illustrious Patronage, and with whom (during the Short Period of his Life) he lived in the greatest Esteem at Holme-Pierpoint in Nottinghamshire; where being seized with Small-Pox, he was unfortunately taken off the 9th Day of December 1683 in the 30th Year of his Age.

Kingston tried to persuade him to take Holy Orders so that he could become chaplain to his household. But Oldham remained a proud, independent spirit to the end. Besides, he certainly must have retained bitter memories of his own life in the household of a dissident clergyman, and found intolerable the very thought of placing himself at the beck and call of the members of a great family and turning into a clerical toady for the sake of a few creature comforts. In the *Satire Addressed to a Friend That is About to Leave the University*, a work cited earlier as the source of one of the memorable sketches in Macaulay's *History of England*, Oldham examined the few choices of livelihood open to worthy but penniless young men from undistinguished families. There he dismissed the chaplain's life out of hand—the chaplain whose maintenance and future hopes depend on the moods of a noble master:

> Let those that have mind, turn slaves to eat,
> And live contented by another's plate:
> I rate my freedom higher, nor will I
> For food and raiment truck my liberty.

A reader, of course, must make allowance for the hyperbole and the literary antecedents of his satire. Nonetheless, Oldham's vigorous lines are those of an independent-minded man who, despite lack of family and means, was sure of his abilities and too proud to grovel. Rachel Trickett in her study stresses his independence and self-reliance, particularly in an age when poets often had to abase themselves to win the goodwill of an arrogant and wealthy patron. This pride and a sturdy defiance of vicissitude are the qualities that most endear Oldham to a modern reader. His advertisement to his last collection, *Poems and Translations* (1683), is almost a brief manifesto in which he asserts his self-reliance:

This at present is content to come abroad baked, undedicated, and unprefac'd, without one kind word to shelter it from censure; and so let the critics take it amongst them.

Details of Oldham's life after 1681 are scarce. We have already noted his abortive attempt at the study of medicine while he was tutor to the son of Sir William Hicks. We know, too, that he declined the opportunity to accompany his pupil on the Grand Tour. Whether he tried his hand at making a literary career on his own between his leaving the service of the Hicks family and taking up final residence at the Earl of Kingston's estate at Holme-Pierrepoint is uncertain. It is obvious, however, that he had come to be regarded as a writer of both promise and achievement. He was commissioned to compose the ode for the second annual commemoration of the feast of St. Cecilia, the patroness of music, a celebration which was started on November 22, 1683. This ode, "An Ode for the Anniversary of Music on St. Cecilia's Day," was set to music by the highly respected musician Dr. John Blow for the 1684 celebration of the feast, a year after the poet's death. The title page of the text and score, published in 1685 as *A Second Musical Entertainment Perform'd on St. Cecilia's Day*, lists as the author of the work "the late ingenious Mr. John Oldham." Brooks conjectures that Oldham may have written the work in the last two weeks of his life.

The ode, irregular in form, is little more than a stock academic exercise, marked by overworked comparisons and tributes to music's power—"the cordial of a troubled breast," "the softest remedy that grief can find." The several references to death and what waits beyond the grave supply a poignant note for a reader in view of the youthful and luckless poet's impending fate—

> Without the sweets of melody,
> To tune our vital breath
> Who would not give it up to death,
> And in the silent grave contented lie?

Fittingly, there was irony in his fate, for, as Brooks remarks,

just as his gift was maturing and his prospects brightening, he died of smallpox. . . .[22]

Like his mentor Rochester, Oldham felt it necessary to repent of whatever looseness of living he was guilty. Anthony Wood's fussy disapproval of his way of life, a censure that so exercised the writer of the memoirs, may have had some warrant. The memoirist's defense of Oldham against the charge of debauchery rests on the grounds that the work that outraged Wood and other contemporary readers, the *Satire Against Virtue*, was without the poet's knowledge printed and included in an edition of Rochester's obscene poems. In any event, Oldham's *Letter to an Old Friend*, written after he had left London— the tone of which, by the way, is instructive in that it conveys his pleasant manner and essentially good nature—contains expressions of sorrow at having been "an unconcerned coxcomb" at one time. Experience taught him that only "virtue and sobriety (how much soever the men of wit turn 'em into ridicule)" can lead to true happiness, while not ruling out "briskness, aeriness, and gayety."

Printed along with Oldham's *Remains* in 1684 was a prose piece entitled *A Sunday Thought in Sickness* in which the poet repented of his sins and confessed his faith. Facing the prospect of death, he admits:

How have I abused and misemployed those parts and talents which might have rendered me serviceable to mankind, and repaid an interest of glory to their donor!

In a moving passage, he asks why he fears to leave this life:

Neither is it that I'm loth to leave the delights and pleasures of the world; some of them I've tried, and found empty, the others covet not, because unknown. I'm confident I could despise 'em all by greatness of soul, did not the Bible tell me, and divines tell me, 'tis my duty. It is not neither that I'm willing to go hence before I've established a reputation, and something to make me survive myself.

Despite the harshness of his life and his losing struggle to make his way as an independent writer, he did manage within a pitifully short

lifetime to leave something that survived himself. He left his mark
on English satire, as it is the purpose of this study to show, and won
the respect of many of his contemporaries.

An engraving of him appeared in the first volume of *The Biographical Mirror* (London, 1795). Reprinted for the modern student
in the second volume of Yale University Press's edition of *Poems on
Affairs of State* (1965), a work to be referred to frequently in succeeding chapters, it shows him to have been somewhat as his memoirist
described him, a rather thin-faced young man, with long, narrow
nose and full lips. Although appropriately serious-looking, his whole
bearing and mien hint at a whimsical, pleasant disposition. The engraving shows someone a modern student would like to know more
about. It is reprinted as the frontispiece of this study.

Chapter Two

"Setting Up for a Wit"

We have already noted how some of his poems brought Oldham the good opinion of the ruling clique of wits. Again, as noted in passing in Chapter 1, a poem like the obscene *Sardanapalus* was even attributed to the Earl of Rochester and included in early editions of his work. David Vieth, editor of *The Complete Poems of John Wilmot* (1968) has argued in an article that the *Satire Against Virtue*, an exercise in wit, is the work that really brought Oldham to Rochester's attention. The basis for this claim is a statement prefixed to a manuscript copy of the satire in the Osborne collection at Yale University.[1]

What is of significance is that Oldham did indeed "set up for a wit," in Anthony Wood's ill-tempered phrase, and, as we have noted, took Rochester as one of his models. The more than three-hundred-page manuscript in the Bodleian Library contains autograph copies of Rochester's *Satire Upon Mankind* and *Letter from Artemisa*. But as indicated earlier, this in itself by no means establishes that the two poets were ever closely associated, just as the fact that the same collection contains parts of Dryden's *MacFlecknoe* in autograph does not establish any relationship between the two poets concerned. (For that matter, Professor Brooks lists in his *Bibliography* a 1709 edition of *MacFlecknoe* printed along with Oldham's *With Spenser's Ghost*, and it has been argued elsewhere that Oldham is really the author of the former work.)[2] All we can conclude with certainty is that Oldham had the highest regard for both Dryden and Rochester. The latter, as we have noted, he called "an incomparable person" in the preface to his *Poems and Translations* (1684). He set out to emulate them both by becoming a satirist and a wit. In fact, Oldham was awarded his place as a satirist alongside Rochester and Dryden by his contemporaries. Yet a reader of the verse epistle *A Letter from the Country to a Friend in Town* can only conclude that Rochester and Oldham were more than just admirers of each other's work. It seems likely that the friend addressed, someone who has praised the author for his talent

even as the author bewails his own devotion to poetry as a pursuit
of "the worst of Jilts," is none other than the talented earl—

> We guess what proofs your genius would impart
> Did it employ you, as it does divert.

Like Rochester, Oldham imitated the ancients, leaned toward the indecent and obscene, cursed and abused enemies mercilessly. The two
often drew upon the same sources: both imitated the Roman satirists,
and both imitated Boileau (although "imitated" must be carefully
qualified in this instance, since the two Englishmen and the French-
man were drawing upon common sources). In addition, both delighted
in upsetting conventional notions of morality, and both wrote to please
the same audiences.

Intellectual Ironist: *The Satire Against Virtue*

The Satire Against Virtue well supports Oldham's claim to some
standing as a wit. It is one of his better attempts at the Pindaric ode,
a form popularized at the time by Abraham Cowley, a poet Oldham
greatly admired and whose Horatian imitations he knew well. His admiration for the older poet was so strong that he boasted in a 1681
collection of his works, *Some New Pieces*, to know "the beloved Cowley by heart." Unfortunately, he suffered from "the unskillful touch"
which Cowley himself said the Pindaric form cannot endure. He certainly played no part in vivifying the Pindaric as a genre. His failings
and successes with the form will be discussed in some detail later on.

Although Oldham is no match for Rochester in licentiousness of
matter, felicity of expression, smoothness of cadence or rhyme, or in
intellectual irony, his *Satire Against Virtue* is a good example of his
wit, taking "wit" in the general sense of the philosopher Thomas
Hobbes, who in *Human Nature* (1650) defined it simply as an
"agility of spirit." The satire is in a vein that reached its point of
highest development in the next century with the sustained and devastating irony of a work like Jonathan Swift's *Argument Against the
Abolition of Christianity* (1708). No matter how maladroit Oldham's handling of the Pindaric form, the unfolding of his ironic argument is cleverly managed. Within the purely decorative pattern of
the Pindaric strophe, antistrophe, and epode, he builds an elaborate
tongue-in-cheek argument that conforms to the rules laid down by

Renaissance rhetoricians who, following Cicero, divided a composition into six parts: the exordium, the narrative, the partition, the confirmation, the refutation, and the peroration.

It may seem a gratuitous bit of pedantry to bring such antiquarian impedimenta into the interpretation of a poem that can be read by a general reader with a good deal of enjoyment. Yet awareness of these formal elements helps a reader appreciate how Oldham's irony operates. For that matter, he based others of his odes on the same rhetorical model, e.g., *The Praise of Homer* and *A Dithyrambic on Drinking*. In so doing, he was carrying on a convention going back to the Greeks and the Romans, a convention usually associated with high and serious argument, although Erasmus had shown how it could be used with powerful satiric effect in his *Praise of Folly*. Put simply, the carefully organized argument permits a reader to accept for the moment what is condemned by any right-thinking person. Thus shock and moral outrage are tempered by amusement. In the hands of the greatest satirists—Swift or Fielding, for example—an ostensible encomium of principles that turn the universe of moral values upside down can convey profound and memorable moral lessons.

Oldham begins his *Satire Against Virtue* by inducing in the reader a proper and receptive frame of mind, which is the function of the *exordium*. Presuming upon the reader's agreement with the fictional persona who speaks in the ode, he levels a rousing curse at all those who "fetter" us with rules of conduct and religion. How enviable is the lot of the beasts—

> More happy beasts: who the great rule of sense
> observe. Happy whose lives are merely to enjoy.

Human virtue should be sent off packing to "those airy mansions rare" and awarded "converse" with the saints. Only someone who is all "soul"—and who among us mortals is?—could really practice it. Does history, for that matter (and here the ironic argument moves into the *narratio*, or narrative, section), contain a record of anyone who ever really profited by courting virtue? The silence that greets such a question can only confirm the poet's stand. Socrates was rewarded with a cup of hemlock for his stout adherence to virtue.

Nonetheless, there are some who do respect virtue, the speaker grudgingly admits in a section that cleverly presents the *partition* of the topic, wherein the area of agreement is marked off from the area of dispute. Let older people respect the idea of virtue if they will. As for him, he says,

> I have not yet the leisure to be good.

And nothing will do but for him to revile the common arguments for leading the good life. Peace of mind, for example? That, and pleasure besides, can be found in "wine and company." Fear of an accusing conscience? This is little more than the "vain fantastic fear" of punishments that we are not even certain will arrive, punishments devised by cunning statesmen and priests ("gown'd impostors") to awe "slavish" ordinary men. The road to happiness can be traveled only by those who sin bravely (a side thrust, perhaps, at the Lutheran doctrine of justification by faith alone) and thus earn everlasting renown:

> A true and brave transgressor ought
> To sin with the same height of spirit Caesar fought.

Only look at great Jove himself, who . . .

> heav'n one large seraglio made:
> Each goddess turns into a glorious punk of the trade.

This reference to Jove brings the argument to the *confirmation*, or proof, of the speaker's position. Can there be any doubt about what history proves? The proof contains in itself the *refutation* wherein it is demonstrated how cowardly is the position of those who embrace virtue. Greatness is achieved through evil. The list of those who have won undying fame by burning and destroying cities alone makes up an epic catalog, from Hector, to Nero, to Guy Fawkes. The thought of burning and fire leads to thoughts of Lucifer himself who, as Oldham notes in a line with a strong and appropriate Miltonic echo,

> Condemn'd that Heaven, where he could not reign.

The *peroration*, or conclusion of the argument, reaches a rousing climax. The boisterous speaker sums up his argument for the greatness of evil by asserting confidently that the moral philosophers have been hoodwinking gullible men for centuries. But he and fellow spirits of

truly heroic mold are not part of the common herd for whom, in the
formula of the Scholastic philosophers Oldham must have learned
at Oxford,

> sin is but a mere privative of good.

Instead, like the pioneering scientists and scholars of the Royal Society
of Arts and Sciences chartered by Charles II not too long before, in
1662,

> We are the Royal Society of vice
> Whose talents are to make discoveries,
> And advance sin like other arts and sciences.

Lines like these even suggest the deliberate cultivation of the diabolic
by Rochester and his circle, as well as suggest the rant of the contemporary heroic plays. In fact, the peroration comes to its thundering climax with the speaker expressing his disappointment at not
having the opportunity given Cain to perform a monumentally evil
act. If so, he boasts,

> I'd done some great and unexampled deed. . . .
> And show that sin admits transcendency.

The *Satire Against Virtue* seems so self-conscious and carefully
staged a performance that one agrees with David Vieth that Oldham
must have written it with his eye on the favor and approbation of
Rochester and his associates. The work contains the audacity—or, better
yet, the insolence—and boldness of invention that must have appealed
to them. Oldham, in fact, used as epigraph for his poem some lines
from Juvenal's first satire which can be translated freely as follows:
dare to do something bold enough to earn you a prison term, if you
really want to be someone (*Aude aliquid brevibus Gyaris et carcere
dignum, si vis esse aliquid*). Whether the tag refers to his own dar-
ing in publishing a satire bound to scandalize some or to Rochester's
notorious conduct is a matter for conjecture. Indeed, a prefatory note
attached to the satire in editions of the poet's collected works, besides
striking a modern reader as disingenuous and unworthy of the author,
indicates that the satire was intended as a *jeu d'esprit*, meant only for

the eyes of a few friends. Because of the amoral tone of the satire, Oldham apparently wanted to disclaim any intention of championing vice at the expense of virtue, explaining that the work was

...meant to abuse those who valued themselves upon their wit and parts in praising vices; At first he intended it not for the public, nor to pass beyond the privacy of two or three friends.

As indicated earlier, the *Satire Against Virtue* was one of Oldham's works that circulated in manuscript. Anthony Wood noted in an entry of his *Athenae Oxonienses* for 1679 that the

Satire against Virtue was committed to the privacy of two or three friends from whose hands it stole out into print against the author's knowledge.[3]

Once it had been published, the author, understandably, felt it should at least be in print unmarred by the errors of earlier copies and unauthorized printings.

Still, there is no evidence that Oldham was in any real sense depraved or vicious. Yet his protestations of repentance for the immoral tone of his attempts at playing the wit contain a somewhat false ring. It seems apparent that in the *Satire Against Virtue* he deliberately set out to challenge conventional notions of morality. The satire, despite its hyperbole and its straining for effect, deserves critical attention in its own right. Parts of it stand up well when compared with verses of Rochester in the same vein. Most readers will agree with Brooks when he states that

one can see...why it was the *Satire Against Virtue* that Pope listed among the 'most Remarkable Works in this Author.

No matter how tedious the elaborate rhetorical trappings may seem to the modern reader, there is an element of authentic wit in the satire, in particular, as Brooks notes in the essay just cited,

in the sophistical attack on the impregnable defence of the indefensible.[4]

No doubt, the satire had the greatest impact on contemporary readers who were aware, as the 1679 printing indicated in the long title, that it was "supposed to be spoken by a Town Hector," that is, by someone like Rochester whose exploits were known throughout the town.

The *Satire Against Virtue* leaves one wondering if Oldham ever really did consider taking Holy Orders, and, on the other hand, if his having grown up in the household of a dissenting clergyman prevented him from seriously flouting the conventional standards of morality. In any event, he later wrote an apology, which is included in editions of his works, and even composed a *Counterpart to the Satire Against Virtue*, which was published with his *Remains*. The latter piece, a Pindaric of nine stanzas spoken "in the person of the author," is undistinguished, filled with platitudes and conventional apostrophes to virtue, of which the following stands as a representative sample:

> Soft gentle yoke!
> Best mistress of our souls!

Nonetheless, the commonplace quality and overall mediocrity of this recantation cannot quite hide the character and strength of mind of the poet. There is a strain of stoicism in some of the verses that commands the reader's attention:

> Grant me, Virtue, thy most solid lasting joy,
> Grant me the better pleasures of the mind,
> Pleasures, which only in pursuit of thee we find,
> Which fortune cannot mar, nor chance destroy.

Although Bell omitted in his edition the work that prompted it, he does, as might be expected, include the edifying *Counterpart*. He felt compelled, however, to supply a rather lengthy footnote to explain the omission of the original satire. It deserves quotation in part:

If Oldham found it necessary to deprecate its [i.e., the *Satire Against Virtue*] coarseness at a time when no language was considered too gross for satire, there is still greater reason for rejecting it altogether in the present age. It may be inferred . . . that had he lived to revise and collect his works, he would himself have cast out a foolish poem which he earnestly regretted having written. The satire comes strictly within Pope's censure [of some of Oldham's poems]. It is mere bald Billingsgate and falls flat from the dead weight of its gratuitous extravagance. Oldham mistook his powers when he attempted a masquerade of this kind, which requires to be sustained by the play of covert wit. His strength was in the opposite direction; and he always succeeded best when he went straight to his object.[5]

Although prompted by Victorian squeamishness, this, as we shall have occasion to see, is nonetheless a fair assessment of Oldham's strength as a satirist.

Trying to Cut a Rakish Figure

Another glimpse of the kinds of figures Rochester and his companions must have cut at times, so like the ranting characters of the late seventeenth-century heroic drama in their defiance of the code by which ordinary mortals live, is provided by Oldham's *Dithyrambic on Drinking*, which the prudish Robert Bell, it is amusing to note, insists was really "a masked attack" on one of the fashionable vices of the times. Whether this was the poet's real intention or not, the drunken ranting of the poem's speaker reminds us inevitably of Rochester—and his confession to Bishop Burnet on the occasion of his conversion to virtue and religion before he died. It will be recalled that he told the Bishop that in one period of his life he was drunk "for five years together."

This work is not a dithyramb in the stricter sense of Dryden's famous *Alexander's Feast*, which is organized around a series of elaborate strophes and choruses. Rather, it is one by virtue of its being filled with exaggerations and enthusiasm. The concluding stanza, indeed, is little less than a "torrent" of hyperbole in its call for a "torrent" of drink:

> Oh, what a torrent of drink have we,
> Bring, bring a deluge, fill us up to the sea,
> Let the vast sea be our mighty cup,
> We'll drink it, and also its fishes too, like loaches up.

These lines and the entire dithyramb suffer when compared with these stanzas from Rochester's much more elegant *Upon His Drinking a Bowl*:

> Vulcan, contrive me such a cup
>   As Nestor used of old.
> Show all thy skill to trim it up;
>   Damask it round with gold.

> Make it so large that, filled with sack
> Up to the swelling brim,
> Vast toasts on the delicious lake
> Like ships at sea may swim.

There is, however, a definite line of argument in Oldham's dithyramb and a recognizable trace of the structure of the classical rhetorical composition. The wit of the effort inheres in an impertinent turning of the moral universe topsy-turvy. Canting divines, so the argument goes, have long deceived men with their warnings against the evils of alcohol. But the speaker, someone of truly heroic mold, will not be hoodwinked: "It is resolved, I will drink on, and die." And why not? With every "gulp" we "life's tedious journey shorter make." Sober reason is the "fond disturber of our life." Wine alone can inspire us with the frenzy and madness that fill the prophet.

This systematic and witty standing of the normal order on its head is worth looking at in some detail, if only to see how the poem achieves its effect. In the opening stanza the speaker establishes his credentials by telling us that he is no "inexperienced fop," new to the virtues of drink and ripe for the guile of the divines. Rather, a drinker of long standing, he is well aware of "the worth" of drunkenness and wine:

> I've tried, and proved, and found it all divine.

The stanza that follows announces that the drunkard is not a slave to life like the "vile slaves of business," but is someone who knows how to make life's tiresome journey shorter and live like the gods who laugh at human woe. Surely the gods must drink, for without liquor there could be no paradise—a consideration which leads to an apostrophe to the grape (stanza 3), the inspirer of men, the maker of poets who begat the gods and challenged the mighty Alexander to drink as well as to conquer.

The way to the good life, then, is to measure out the hours by drink (stanza 4). Noah was a true "second father of mankind," for it was he who after the Flood "durst be drunk again, and with new vice the world replant" (stanza 5). The wise man bids farewell to reason, a disturbing element in our lives, and welcomes a higher madness and frenzy—

> A more exalted noble faculty,
> Above thy logic, and vain boasted pedantry.

Thus, the next-to-the-last stanza leads into the last, which reaches a peak of truly heroic rant with a summons to stay drunk and

> march off, and reel into the tomb,
> Nature's convenient and dark retiring-room;
> And there, from noise removed, and all tumultuous strife,
> Sleep out the dull fatigue, and long debauch of life.

Although a modern reader is not surprised to find a Victorian editor like Bell looking for morally redeeming qualities in a work of this kind, his assertion that the "bombastic fury that pervades it [the *Dithyrambic*] is the very essence of ridicule" still strikes us as simple-minded and prudish self-deception. True enough, even though when he wrote the poem Oldham was living the sheltered school-master's life in Croydon, he was certainly aware that excessive drinking was one of the more vicious practices of the age. It is also true, as Bell notes, that

Etherege, Rochester, or Sedley might have sat for the portrait, and were probably the actual originals from which it was drawn. They were as notorious for their excesses in this way, as Dryden for his temperance, and Waller for water-drinking.[6]

Given Oldham's awareness of the vices of the time and the Court, a reader detects a double-edged quality in the poem: a witty encom-ium on a fashionable and vicious way of life in a difficult and un-settled period, along with a covert warning to devotees of the bottle.

The *Dithyrambic*, in fact, contains some good lines, especially the final ones quoted above. Despite the rant and fustian which grate on modern ears and sensibilities, the work is a worthy addition to the long line of rousing poems, reaching from Greek lyricists through medieval Latin writers, celebrating the virtues of drink.

To be considered along with the *Dithyrambic* is Oldham's "A Careless Good Fellow," a much more mellow effort that Bell also admitted to his edition. The seven six-line stanzas of the song contain an authentic note of resignation to the evils of the age. They also display one of Oldham's characteristic mannerisms, that of donning one of two masks when addressing himself to the evils of the times. On some occasions, as we shall see when examining his best-known and most sustained effort at topical satire, the *Satires Upon the Jesuits*, he puts on the mask of a stern, outraged English Juvenal launching a savage frontal assault on evil, a verbal barrage marked by violent denunciation, invective, and scatological abuse. On other occasions he wears the mask of ironist, although, sadly, too often much of his irony tends to sink under its own weight.

"The Careless Good Fellow" shows him as a gentle and effective ironist, and is, in fact, a memorable expression of the nature of the times in which he lived. What can a reasonable man do, the speaker in the poem asks, but retreat to the enjoyment of the bottle, refusing to bother his head about such matters as plots, questions as to who should succeed to the throne once Charles is gone, the puzzle as to who is allied with whom in the confusing military campaigns on the Continent? The opening lines have the abrupt and crusty manner of the Roman satirist, the manner that Swift and Pope were to master so well in the next century:

> A plague of all this fooling and plotting of late,
> What a pother and stir has it kept in the State;
> Let the rabble run mad with suspicions and fears,
> Let them scuffle and jar, till they go by the ears;
> Their grievances never shall trouble my pate,
> So I can enjoy my dear bottle at quiet.

This short piece succeeds in capturing the confusion, shock, and general disillusionment of the ordinary citizen as each day in those troubled times brought fresh reports of alleged plots on the king's life and intrigues surrounding the matter of succession to the throne, while taxes became ever more burdensome, to the point that the speaker finds it more and more expensive to seek solace in his beloved wine:

> Yet oft in my drink I can hardly forbear
> To curse them for making my claret so dear.

Yet, despite his cavalier and cynical attitude toward the current political and religious intrigue—

Come he [i.e., the King of France], or the pope, or the devil to boot,
Or come faggot and stake, I care not a groat—

he is fearful and genuinely concerned about the threat to order in the
kingdom. The last two lines make this clear:

I'll drink in defiance of gibbet and halter,
This is the profession that never will alter.

The tone of gentle resignation is all the more effective when we
remember that the author was the very same man who launched a
vicious frontal attack on the Pope and his legions of Jesuits in the
Satires Upon the Jesuits. The times must have been trying, indeed,
for the patriotic Protestant Englishman.

Still another poem that may very well have earned Oldham the
notice of the Wits, and Rochester in particular, is "The Dream,"
mentioned earlier in connection with his pornographic efforts. It is
dated March 10, 1677, in early editions of the works. The subject
is an erotic dream, and is reminiscent of the work of Rochester,
although without explicit indecency. Of most interest to a modern
reader is the basic premise of the poem, the notion of the woman's
natural depravity and lechery, a doctrine inherited from classical antiquity and honored by the wits, rakes, and preachers of Oldham's
and later ages. The woman's resistance to masculine assault and her
seeming modesty are purely ceremonial, her apparent refusal only
the mask for an invitation:

Ah, do not, do not, do not—let me go.

Oldham, too, gives this rather embarrassing effort a somewhat
blasphemous ending, with puns and double entendres calculated to
please readers like Rochester. Describing his dream, he writes, stress-
ing "dying" with its double meaning:

Not dying saints enjoy such ecstacies
When they in vision antedate their bliss.

He knew how to write in a way to please the Wits.

Satirist at Heart

If Oldham's reputation rested solely on the works just discussed, he would soon have been forgotten. These poems are of interest, for the most part, in that they supply a picture of a bright and talented young man trying to make his way in the literary world. Not unlike scores of other young men who came to London in search of fame and fortune, he sought the approval and support of those whose goodwill could advance his career. Unluckily for him, however, he lacked skill as an ironist and ran too easily to bluster and rant, as is demonstrated, say, in the *Dithyrambic Against Drinking.* One of his most serious failings as a writer and satirist was that he lacked the lightness of touch and inventiveness of approach to make the unseemly and indecent amusing rather than disgusting. It must also be kept in mind, of course, that pieces like the *Dithyrambic* and the *Satire Against Virtue* are in conventions that were well known to contemporary readers. Oldham's efforts must have suffered by comparison with examples of ironic praise of the unpraiseworthy, or celebrations of the blameworthy, like Samuel Butler's *"Pindarick Ode to the Memory of the Most Renowned Dick Vale"* (1671), written in honor of a notorious highwayman, or some of Rochester's elegantly turned drinking songs.

Oldham's real talent was for invective and the direct attack. Rachel Trickett tells us that he had great respect for Persius, a Roman poet much admired in the sixteenth and seventeenth centuries, whose satire ran to violence and harshness of tone. This admiration is reflected in what must have been another of the attempts to curry the favor of Rochester and his circle, the *Satire Upon a Woman*, a sample of concentrated abuse that comes dangerously close to becoming a *reductio ad absurdum* of its genre. Written in the already well-established "curse" tradition of the time, the satire exacts revenge from a woman whose heartlessness has resulted in the death of the poet's friend, a not uncommon situation in attacks on women:

> I rise in judgment, am to be to her
> Both witness, judge, and executioner
> Arm'd with dire satire, and resentful spite,
> I come to haunt her with the ghosts of wit—

whereupon the "ghosts of wit" rise to wish upon her every known or imagined variety of physical and moral evil.

Unfortunately for the patient reader, the nastiness is not relieved or lightened by cleverness of invention or neatness of expression, a deficiency also of another attempt to haunt with the "ghosts of wit," a poem with the long (and explicit) title, *Upon a Lady who by overturning of a coach, had her coats behind her flung up, and was under shown to the view of the company.* The situation depicted needs no further description. Despite a touch here and there of cleverness, the poem remains essentially a nasty joke.

Oldham, however, cannot be dismissed as little more than an ambitious young man of some talent trying to make his way in the world by a fashionable flouting of the public sense of decorum and decency. In much of his work, of course, he was mining what was then in vogue, especially the satiric conventions stemming from the ancients. Yet even when he is consciously and openly imitating a Roman satirist, the reader is aware that he is more than satirist *manqué*, but is a genuine satiric spirit who in his heart scorned the Grub Street necessity of fawning upon the rich and the powerful. In his version of one of Boileau's satires he was to convey eloquently his disgust for the ways of the world. Even though his work is not an imitation as the term "imitation" came to be understood, containing as it does, only a few up-to-date applications, its controlling idea, the worthlessness of glittering ancestry, titles, patents of nobility, comes through with a ring of sincerity:

> Cursed be the day, when first this vanity
> Did primitive simplicity destroy,
> In the blessed state of infant time, unknown,
> When glory sprung from innocence alone;
> Each from his merit only title drew,
> And that alone made kings, and nobles too,
> But merit, by degenerate time at last,
> Saw vice ennobled, and herself debased;
> And haughty pride false pompous titles feigned,
> To amuse the world, and lord it o'er mankind.

True, this is a complaint voiced by the ancients, who liked to hearken back to a lost Golden Age of mankind before men had been corrupted by wealth and power. Yet in view of what we knew of Oldham's life and career, we feel that he speaks from the heart when he bemoans a world grown so depraved that "zeal for honor" no longer characterizes the aristocracy, rather

> 'Tis now thought mean, and much beneath a lord
> To be an honest man, and keep his word. . . .

We have already noted how, at the end of his life, in the prose meditation "A Sunday-Thought in Sickness," while repenting of his shortcomings, Oldham assures us that he was never taken in by the world and its glitter. All in all, despite his attempts to play the wit, a modern reader is willing to accept his claim to a "greatness of soul."

All this is not to overlook the fact that Oldham did earn a reputation for "lewdness" that outlived him. It is interesting to note that the *Gentleman's Magazine* in 1732 contained an essay on modesty which eventually got around to a discussion of lewdness in writers. Although Oldham is not listed with those "most eminently criminal this way"—among them, Prior and Rochester—he is awarded a place with writers among whom "slips are to be found." The latter group includes distinguished people: "Shakespeare, Johnson, Denham, Etheridge . . . and Steele."

There is good reason to believe that Oldham deserved to be called an "English Juvenal." He was not cut out for a wit. Rather, he was of a philosophic turn of mind and wrote invective and vituperation because the depravity of the society in which he lived left him no other choice. The "Careless Good Fellow," the already discussed drinking song that he wrote in 1680 after the frenzy of the Popish Plot had reached its peak—a frenzy he himself had helped inspire through his *Satires Upon the Jesuits*—bespeaks the disenchantment and resignation of a genuine satirist. As noted above, he must have tired of the madness of the Plot, the endless machinations of the papists, the shameful treaties with the Dutch, the bullying of Louis XIV on the Continent. The temptation for the thoughtful man to withdraw into himself and turn to friends and a glass of wine must have been strong:

> Their grievances never shall trouble my pate
> So I can enjoy my dear bottle at quiet.

But it was not in Oldham's nature to enjoy a "dear bottle" at quiet for very long. As W. J. Courthope in his *History of English Poetry* remarks judiciously, Oldham was "consumed by two master passions . . . love of independence and love of poetry."[7]

His fierce sense of independence made him seek out the fray, particularly in struggles that involved religion and country. His instinct
for the direct assault and his great powers of invective encouraged him
to seek out worthy targets. It was as a political satirist that he found
his biggest game.

Chapter Three

The Art of Political Satire

An Age of Bitter Satire

The second half of the reign of Charles II, during the years from 1674 to 1685, was a stormy time in English political and social life. The historian Maurice Ashley sums up the character of the age as follows:

So deep was the confusion, so wild the passions of the time that only by an ace was civil war to be averted in the last years of his reign and the King allowed to die in Whitehall instead of once more in exile.[1]

The enmity between Cavalier and Puritan did not lessen. A Court party grew up in opposition to a Country party. The two parties—from which sprang the "Whigs" and the "Tories"—knew no bounds in their use of libel and vilification. The members of the Court party were often dependent for their rank and livelihood on the king, the Established Church, and the Stuart line of succession. The opposition party embraced those whose instincts were republican, and who saw in the Duke of York's eventual succession to the throne a likely return to papistry and tyranny.

The name Whig—a term of obscure origin, but thought to be a shortening of "Whiggamore," which, according to the *Concise Oxford Dictionary*, was the name applied to the group of Scottish dissenters who marched on Edinburgh in 1684—was attached to the rapier-tongued and quick-witted Earl of Shaftesbury who was pressing boldly and recklessly for a parliamentary act that would exclude the professedly Catholic York from succeeding his brother, who himself, according to reports from informed contemporaries, was secretly a Catholic while he lived and openly one as he lay dying.

A Tory—a term which seems to have meant originally an Irish robber—was a member of the vaguely defined group "founded" in a sense by Charles's powerful Lord Treasurer Danby. Despite their support of the Established Church and their unremitting attempts to thwart the Catholicizing tendencies of the king, the Tories never wavered in their loyalty to the hereditary monarchy. For that matter, the fears on both sides of a return to Catholicism were far from groundless. James, the Duke of York, was an avowed Catholic as early as 1670. With the indiscretion that characterized him throughout his life, he also asserted that his brother King Charles intended to become a Catholic and bring the nation back into the Roman fold.

Compounding and exacerbating the fear and suspicion that made the times so uneasy was the abiding hatred Englishmen of all classes felt for the French. Understandably, because of his years of exile in France, Charles felt great sympathy with France and the French. In the words of John Kenyon, a recent historian of the Popish Plot, Louis XIV had taken on the role of "popish bogeyman" last played by Philip II of Spain until his death in 1598. Coupled with disclosures of the numbers of Roman Catholics holding important positions in the army and serving in other high places, despite the long-standing requirement that anyone holding governmental office take an oath recognizing the king's supremacy over the Pope in the English Church, Charles's ties to the French king were persuading both the Commons and ordinary citizens that popery was, indeed, on the rise. Unknown to the public, the king's involvement was even deeper. The Treaty of Dover between England and France, signed in May 1670, contained a secret clause committing Charles to an announcement of his conversion, while Louis XIV pledged military help in controlling the ensuing public response. As students of the period know, the king was given to such deviousness and duplicity.

But unfortunately for his English sympathizers and their king, Louis XIV's grand dynastic designs, his military adventuring, his diplomatic chicanery, his bewildering and ceaseless forming and dissolving of alliances were upsetting the balance of power on the Continent. Charles continued to play his devious game, his most disreputable move being a series of secret deals with the French king in return for which he was paid cash subsidies. Inflamed by the tireless and fearless gadfly Shaftesbury, who succeeded in skillfully exploiting the nation's deeply ingrained dread of a return to popery, Parliament stood firm in its determination to support all who opposed Louis. In the historian Ashley's words:

... seldom in English history was the foreign policy of the executive so much at variance with the wishes of parliament.[2]

When at a climactic moment in 1678, the horrifying details of the Popish Plot against the king's life were dramatically revealed to the English public by the unspeakable Titus Oates—the plot that was to provide the subject of Oldham's most sustained and savage effort at satire, the *Satires Upon the Jesuits*—a politician as shrewd and unscrupulous as the Whig leader Shaftesbury saw a rare opportunity to deny the crown to the Duke of York. Whether Shaftesbury believed Oates's revelations to any degree, or simply regarded him as a rascal and a liar, the view shared by most historians, is beside the point. He determined to seize opportunity by the forelock and became thereafter the relentless investigator of the affair in Parliament, thereby emerging as a staunch defender of the Protestant faith. Dryden summed the matter up memorably for posterity in the following lines in *Absalom and Achitophel*:

> The wish'd occasion of the Plot he takes:
> Some circumstances finds, but more he makes.
>
> (ll. 208–9)

Bishop Gilbert Burnet, although he was to become a prominent Whig, reports the conclusions of a calm and intelligent contemporary observer in his *History of My Own Time*, the first volume of which was published in 1724:

Here was matter enough to work on the fears and apprehensions of the nation; so it is not to be wondered at, if parliaments were hot, and jurists were easy in . . . prosecution.[3]

The rivalry between Whigs and Tories came to a head. With fear of Catholic invasion in the air, whether it were to come from France, Ireland, or Spain, the Whigs were in a position to brand their political opponents agents of the Pope. Shaftesbury constantly reminded his fellow countrymen that "popery and slavery go hand in hand." The Tory response was equally fierce. They had only to remind Englishmen of the murder of the king's father, Charles I. The contemporary descriptions of the two parties which follow are representative of the level of verbal abuse of the times:

A Tory is a monster with an English face, a French heart and an Irish conscience. A creature of a large forehead, prodigious mouth, supple hams and no brains. They are a sort of wild boars, that would root out the constitution . . . that with dark lantern policies would at once blow up the two bulwarks of our freedom, Parliaments and juries; making the first only a Parliament of Paris, and the latter but mere tools to echo back the pleasure of the judge. They are so certain that monarchy is *jure divino* that they look upon all people living under aristocracies or democracies to be in a state of damnation; and fancy that the Grand Seignor, the Czar of Muscovy and the French King dropped down from Heaven with crowns on their heads, and that all their subjects were born with saddles on their backs.

As for the Whig:

His principles are like chaos, a gallimaufry of negatives. He talks of nothing but new light and prophecy, spiritual incomes, indwellings, emanations, manifestations, sealings . . . to which also the zealous twang of his nose adds no small efficacy. He treads the antipodes to everything commanded. . . . This little horn takes a mouth to himself, and his language is Overturn, Overturn. His prayer is a rhapsody of holy hiccups, sanctified barkings, illuminated goggles, sighs, sobs, yexes [belches], gasps and groans. He prays for the King, but with more distinctions and mental reservations than an honest man would have in taking the Covenant.[4]

To savor fully the political climate and the currents of feeling of the time, as well as to place Oldham's *Satires Upon the Jesuits* in proper perspective, the student must turn to a contemporary collection of political satires like *Poems on Affairs of State*, which appeared between 1689 and 1706, and to other indispensable collections like the *Pepys' Ballads* (ed. H. E. Rollins, 1929–32), *Political Ballads of the Seventeenth and Eighteenth Centuries* (ed. W. W. Wilkins, 1860), and the *Roxburghe Ballads* (ed. W. Chapell and J. W. Ebsworth, 1871–97). As is soon made evident by collections of this sort, the factionalism in Oldham's time was almost unbelievably strong and vitriolic. It is, indeed, this very sense of strong factionalism running through some of his work, especially his *Satires Upon the Jesuits*, that makes it difficult for today's general reader to take Oldham seriously as a satirist of interest to ages other than his own. As J. W. Ebsworth notes in the fourth volume of the *Roxburghe Ballads*, one reason Oldham remained largely unread by later generations is that he deliberately made himself the part of a faction, and of a temporary mania.

Anyone who leafs through the recent Yale University edition of *Poems on Affairs of State* (*POAS*), under the general editorship of George deF. Lord, will agree that the partisan feeling was a temporary mania. The second volume of the Yale *POAS* (1965), edited by Elias F. Mengel, Jr., provides modern students with a valuable sample of the verse denouncing papistry, the machinations of some of the Catholic lords, and the licentiousness of a Court notorious for its leanings toward the old religion. The abusive verse, for example, attributed to one Stephen College, a carpenter turned writer who became a denouncer of popery, typifies the mania. It is interesting to note in passing that he also gained renown as the inventor of a weapon called the "Protestant flail," an instrument to be used in chastising the minions of Rome in the kingdom.

Six of the poems attributed to College are reprinted in Yale *POAS* II. One of them, called "A Raree Show," led to his execution in 1681. (A raree show, nowadays called a peep show, was carried around from place to place in a box.) In his poem the unfortunate College represents the king as carrying Parliament throughout England in a box, a reference to the convening of Parliament at Oxford in 1681, in an area traditionally loyal to the king. The lines were to be sung to a tune popular at the time. The opening lines are enough to suggest the rough-and-ready quality of College's talent. (The Topham addressed was the sergeant-at-arms of the House of Commons.)

> Come hither, Topham, come, with a hey, with a hey,
> Bring a pipe and a drum, with a ho;
> Where'er about I go
> Attend my raree show
> With a hey, trany nony nony no.

In another poem, a fierce libel entitled "Truth Brought to Light or Murder Will Out," College attacked the popish lords of the realm. The verse was occasioned in part by the alleged murder by papists of the popular London magistrate Sir Edmund Berry Godfrey, to whom Titus Oates had made his first deposition concerning the horrid Popish Plot. The lords, College charges, are members of

> ...that accursed brood
> Who would convert us by a sea of blood
> And turn the laws of England out of doors....

College's bizarre career as a versifier is of interest in that it suggests the extremes of the times in beliefs, suspicions, and general conduct. After being tried once and acquitted in London, he was put on trial for libel at Oxford, in the same year Charles had summoned Parliament to the Tory stronghold because of the high feeling and tension in London. One Stephen Dugdale, who claimed that certain Catholic lords had attempted to persuade him to murder the king, was a witness against College and testified that the poor carpenter had admitted to writing the libelous "A Raree Show," in which, as already noted, the king is depicted as carrying a puppet Parliament about the countryside as a peep show. Dugdale asserted that College sang the ballad and passed out copies of it to the crowd. The irony of the whole proceeding lay in the fact that at an earlier trumped-up trial, that of Lord Stafford, who had been accused of conspiring with foreign powers to kill the king, the unfortunate College had attested to Dugdale's credibility and respectability as a witness. Despite his vehement denials that he was the author of the libel, the hapless carpenter was doomed. The government was determined to make an example of him before the populace and, accordingly, sentenced him to be hanged, drawn, and quartered on August 31, another victim of the cruel judicial murders of the time. A Tory lampoon ("The Whigs' Lamentation for the Death of Their Dear Brother, the Protestant Joiner"), also reprinted in Yale *POAS* II, saluted the fallen College in these mocking lines:

> Brave College is hang'd, the chief of our hopes,
> For pulling down bishops and making new popes...
> He fram'd a new model to limit the king,
> In hopes crown and scepter might truckle to him.

Then too, to add fuel to the flames of public opinion, there were always the Jesuits, the Pope's "hellish" legions, lurking in the wings, ready to inspire hatred and fear. It was Oldham's mission as a satirist to exploit to the hilt the Protestant fear of them. A ballad printed in the *Roxburghe Ballads*—a ballad, by the way, that was among the anti-papist tracts collected by one of Oldham's contemporaries, the well-known antiquary and anti-papist Narcissus Luttrell—expresses the popular feeling against the Jesuits. "The Jesuits Character," which like other defamatory and libelous ballads of the day was sung to the tune of "Which Nobody Can Deny" (called then "The Blacksmith's Tune"), is unambiguous in its import:

> The doctrine of the devils is all that they teach,
> Woe be to them that come in their reach,
> For murder and treason is all that they preach
> Which nobody can deny....

The tone in which these controversies was carried on, in short, was unbelievably acrimonious and intemperate. Even Dryden himself, whose verse throughout most of *Absalom and Achitophel* demonstrates the judiciousness of his own remark in the foreword that "there's a sweetness in good verse which tickles even while it hurts," could not resist introducing revolting physical details that appall a modern reader as he reads the generally brilliant description of Absalom's (the Duke of Monmouth's) sly counselor Achitophel (Shaftesbury), who like his real-life counterpart was small in stature:

> Of these the false Achitophel was first,
> A name to all succeeding ages curst.
> For close designs and crooked counsels fit;
> Sagacious, bold, and turbulent of wit.
> Restless, unfix'd in principles and place;
> In pow'r unpleas'd, impatient of disgrace.
> A fiery soul which, working out its way,
> Fretted the pygmy body to decay,
> And o'er-informed the tenement of clay.

This is not the place for a recapitulation at third hand of the tangled and tortured history of England from the Restoration to the Glorious Revolution. There is certainly no shortage of general histories of the period, as well as special studies of the principal figures. Those with an interest in the literature of the time and with access to research libraries will discover a wealth of fascinating primary sources—memoirs, letters, diaries. Besides the well-known diaries of Pepys and Evelyn, which are available in popular editions, a serious student can consult contemporary works like the aforementioned Burnet's *History of My Own Time*, Narcissus Luttrell's *Brief His-*

torical Relation of State Affairs from September 1678 to April 1714,
and Sir John Dalrymple's *Memoirs of Great Britain and Ireland.*[5]
For our purposes, that is, examining the political satire of Oldham
and placing in perspective its truly heroic exaggerations, it is enough
to note again that the age was marked by outsized suspicion and
hatred of the French, the Catholics, the Jesuits, and whoever happened to be in an opposing camp. The following lines from a political
satire called *Britannia and Raleigh* (1674–75), written by John
Ayloffe, one of the age's many unremembered satirists, sums up
popular feeling for a modern reader in the abusive language typical
of the time:

> A colony of French possess the court;
> Pimps, priests, buffoons i' th' privy-chamber sport.
> Such slimy monsters ne'er approached a throne
> Since Pharaoh's reign, nor so defil'd a crown.[6]

Before moving on to a consideration of Oldham's contribution to
the political satire of Charles II's reign, it is difficult to resist point-
ing to political parallels in our own time. The inflammatory lampoons
and satires occasioned by Stuart policies suggest the bitterness and
intemperateness of the political divisions of the last half of the
twentieth century. All the late seventeenth-century political and
social scenes lacked was the instant exacerbation provided by the
modern mass media.

Indignation Shapes Our Verse

To most students of English literature, seventeenth-century political
and religious satire, first and foremost, means John Dryden and his
Absalom and Achitophel. In the introduction to the first volume of
Yale *Poems on Affairs of State,* general editor George deF. Lord
states the issue well:

The customary emphasis on Dryden's preeminence coupled with a cor-
responding neglect of his contemporaries confronts us with a strange situation. Dryden towers over a void.[7]

But now that we have the admirable and indispensable Yale *POAS,*
a modern student can no longer be excused for ignoring the less
gifted satirists of Dryden's age. As Lord reminds us in the introduc-

tion just cited: "in quantity and popularity satire stood first among the various kinds of non-dramatic verse written between 1660 and 1714." Although many of the satires and lampoons have not come down to us, having circulated only in manuscript, more than three thousand managed to find their way into print. Lord reports that another twenty-five hundred "State Poems" still exist in manuscript. There were readers both for well-turned courtly verses and for crude partisan attacks. The historian C. V. Wedgewood, after asserting that it was during the reign of Charles II that political satire "comes of age," points to this striking feature of the age:

The contrast between the graceful hyperbole of courtly verse and the ferocious candour of satire was never more marked than in the reign of Charles II when courtly verse was at its most polished and fluent, satire at its most fluent and bitter.[8]

Of the printed pieces that still survive, about twelve hundred were printed in collections that appeared between 1689 and 1716. About thirty such volumes came out, of which *Poems on Affairs of State* was the best known. Between 1689, when it first appeared, and 1707, *POAS* had expanded to four volumes, the nature of the contents changing somewhat from edition to edition. The title page of the fifth edition of 1703, for example, reads as follows:

Poems on Affairs of State: From the Time of Oliver Cromwell to the Abdication of K. James the Second. Written by the Greatest Wits of the Age.

Named among the wits are Buckingham, Rochester, Denham, Marvell, Dryden, and Waller.

Verses included in successive editions cover a wide range of topics, indicative of the broad meaning assigned "Affairs of State." Some dealt with the *amours* of the king and his courtiers; others dealt with purely literary affairs. All, however, shared a freewheeling *ad hominem* approach, mixing furious attacks and heavy invective, and spiced with frequent references to the repugnant attributes and gross physical habits of those under assault. Not all State Poems, however, were abusive. Often, verses addressed to someone an author admired or supported contain the fulsome catalog of the panegyric. At times, a welcome change in an age given over as much to outright abuse as to sycophancy, the panegyric was ironic. For example, one of the satires in Yale *POAS* II entitled "A Panegyric" has as its heroine Nell Gwynne, the king's mistress. It begins with the following mock-heroic lines:

> Of a great heroine I mean to tell,
> And by what just degrees her titles swell,
> To Mrs. Nelly grown from cinder Nell.

Another favorite form was the "Advice" or "Instructions" to a painter, in which an imaginary painter is instructed how to represent a person or an event. This was a form that Edmund Waller established in his panegyric of 1666 on the Duke of York's naval victory over the Dutch at Sole Bay, *Instructions to a Painter, for the Drawing of the Posture and Progress of his Majesty's Forces at Sea.* "Instructions," however, were easily adapted to satiric purposes. Andrew Marvell used the form most notably to denounce the age in his posthumous *Last Instructions to a Painter* (1689).

Modern readers can muster little patience for older and artificial conventional forms, unless they contain ingenious variations on themes of abuse. Thus a Whig satire of 1681, "Advice to the Painter: The Witnesses Against Shaftesbury," reprinted in Yale *POAS* II, catches our attention by going immediately on the attack:

> Painter, draw near, draw here the leering look,
> Of th' bigot bloodhounds when they swore on th' Book. . . .

Other conventional forms—the litany, the vision, the bestiary—were employed for abuse and add much interest to certain of the pieces in *POAS.* All in all, besides reflecting the extremes of spirit that marked the age, the poems reflect honest delight in flaying an opponent. Despite the wide range of political views represented in *POAS,* however, the unknown original editors themselves seem to have shared a republican bias, as is shown by the preface to the fifth edition of 1703, which contains the following statement:

We have therefore reason to hope that the Englishman that is a true lover of his Country's Good and Glory, cannot be displeased at the publishing a Collection, the design of each of which was to remove those pernicious Principles which lead us directly to Slavery. . . .

Englishmen of the Restoration were shaken by real or fancied threats to their liberties as freeborn citizens, as well as by their country's discreditable entanglements in the confusing Continental wars, the machinations of the king's foreign policy, the seeming inroads being made by the Roman Church, and the corruption of parliamentary government. The following doggerel entitled "A Litany," written in 1672 and printed for the first time in Yale *POAS* I, expresses in rough and ready fashion the major concerns of the writers of satires and lampoons:

> From peace with the French and war with the Dutch,
> From a new mouth which will cost us as much,
> And from councils of wits which advise us to such,
> > *Libera nos, Domine.*
>
> From Pope and from priests which lead men astray,
> From fools that by cheats will be so led away,
> From saints that "Go to the Devil" will pray,
> > *Libera nos, Domine.*
>
> From Parliament-sellers elected for ale,
> Who sell the weal public to get themselves bail,
> And if e'er it be dissolved will die in a jail,
> > *Libera nos, Domine.*

This effort bore no title in manuscript, but was headed by this line: "These were written in Lincoln Inn's boghouse/1672." A "boghouse" is a name for a privy—a setting which, as Lord comments, "indicates the ubiquitousness of political expression during these trying times," as well as, one might add, the prevailing level of political humor.[9]

As was noted earlier in connection with the execution of the unfortunate Stephen College, there was good reason for the sizable number of satiric verses that were left in manuscript, including some of Oldham's works. Verse attacks on the king himself became increasingly frequent and bold. Rochester's attacks on the royal person are so filled with obscenities and indecencies as to make quotation in a study of this kind inappropriate. According to contemporary accounts, his "A Satire on Charles II" of 1673, in which, besides mocking the king for his sexual inadequacies, he calls him a "cully," led to his fleeing the Court. His satire became so extreme that it finally earned him the displeasure of a king always willing to in-

dulge the whims and foibles of his favorites, provided they were
seasoned by the spice of wit.

Such attacks were not held back from publication simply because
of their poor taste or because they would have affronted the public
sense of decency. Like some of Oldham's verses, most such satires
made the rounds of the coffeehouses in manuscript and were left
unsigned because the laws against libel were severe. Publication was
subject to both the Treason and Licensing Acts which had been enacted shortly after Charles's return from exile. The first of these acts
made punishable any published writings tending to defame the
monarch, and was stretched to cover writings that circulated in
manuscript. The Licensing Act forbade the printing of materials
contrary to the principles of the Christian faith and subversive of
government. Named licenser of the press was the famous and in-
defatigable pamphleteer, Sir Roger L'Estrange.

Again, this is hardly the place to recount in detail the history of
Restoration suppression of the press, nor is it the place to examine
the career of L'Estrange. Anyone interested in learning more about
the Crown's unsuccessful attempts to suppress libelous and seditious
writings, in print or in manuscript, can be referred, among many
other sources, to the introduction of Yale *POAS* I, histories of Restoration literature, or Alexander Beljame's readable and informative
Men of Letters and the English Public in the Eighteenth Century.
All that we need note here is that a traffic in manuscripts flourished
despite the watchful eyes of the Licensing Office. There was a fairly
profitable business in the transcribing and selling of satires and
lampoons, with the town's coffeehouses serving as steady subscribers.
The unknown author of *Satyr Unmuzzled* (1680), an attack on the
morals of the great which is included in Yale *POAS* II, describes
one way lampoons were distributed. A satirist who is afraid to claim
what he has written, he discloses, would

> ...meanly sneak his lampoons into th' world,
> which are i' th' streets by porters dropp'd and hurl'd.

It is true, of course, that some satires and lampoons were printed
illegally before 1689. But most printed texts date from 1689, when
the new monarchs, William and Mary, were only too willing to
permit criticism of the departed Stuarts, who, even though they had
been discredited, still retained the loyalty of a large part of the nation.

Prurience appeals to readers of all periods, and was appealing to readers of Oldham's time, a time given to extremes in both expression and conduct. Therefore, it is hardly surprising that readers and writers would risk punishment for accounts of the king's and courtiers' sexual exploits and amorous romps in the bedchambers at Court. In particular, the exploits of the notorious George Villiers, the Duke of Buckingham (1628–1687), supplied grist for the satirist's mill, as well as general entertainment to the public of the kind provided nowadays by scandal sheets. Buckingham, the Zimri of *Absalom and Achitophel*, was a man, according to Bishop Burnet, simply devoid of religious sense. He is well described for posterity in "Rochester's Farewell" (1680), a work reprinted in Yale *POAS* II, parts of which have been attributed to Rochester by a modern editor, V. de Sola Pinto, on the basis of internal evidence:

> But when degrees of villainy we name,
> How can we choose but think of Buckingham?
> He who through all of 'em has boldly ran,
> Left ne'er a law unbroke of God or man.
> His treasur'd sin of supererogation
> Swell to a sum enough to damn a nation.

Even in our own age of untrammeled self-expression, the abuse in some of the broadsides of Oldham's time seems excessive, as a genuinely nasty passage from *Satyr Unmuzzled*, the lampoon cited above, demonstrates. The lines attack the much-defamed Nell Gwynne, who was only one of the king's many mistresses:

> Now for a she-buffoon, who, 'tis said,
> Crawl'd into the world without a maidenhead,
> It is most sure 'twas never had by man,
> Nor can she say where it was lost, or when—
> We must conclude she never had one then,[10]

The Popish Plot

One topic that never failed to capture an attentive audience was the fearsome Popish Plot. Fear of the Pope and his minions, of course, went back to Bloody Mary and her reign and, later on, to the national hysteria of Guy Fawkes and the Gunpowder Plot of

1605. For that matter, Catholics had even been accused of setting the Great London Fire of 1666. Titus Oates, one of the chief instigators of the Popish Plot mania, claimed that eighty Jesuits, friars, and priests had started the blaze. Oldham picked up on the charge and in the first of the *Satires Upon the Jesuits* put it into the mouth of the Jesuit Henry Garnett, who urges his fellow to do again what they did—so it was alleged—in 1666:

> Let the fir'd city to your plot give light;
> You raz'd it half before, now raze it quite.

Fears of the popish legions, stirred up by clever propagandists, and the concern over the lack of a Protestant heir to Charles's throne, fueled the anti-Catholic feeling of long standing. When in 1678, Titus Oates, one of recorded history's most prodigious liars, came forward with a highly circumstantial account of a Catholic plot on the life of Charles and a conspiracy to return England to popery on the accession of the Duke of York to the throne, his allegations pushed many Londoners to the brink of hysteria. The Pope, the Jesuits, the Old Church were seen as the source of the country's evils. Soon the whole kingdom was aroused and sharply divided. Anthony Wood, a strong Tory with High Church leanings whose entries and comments are a mine of information for historians, describes how on one occasion the Pope was burnt in effigy at Oxford:

brought out in a chaire, set before the fire, shot at, and then (his belly being full of crackers) was burnt.[11]

Pope-burning, of course, was nothing new. On November 17 of every year the Whigs celebrated Elizabeth's accession to the throne by burning the Pope in effigy. But Oxford, where the Pope-burning described by Wood took place, was a Tory and High Church stronghold.

Everywhere the talk was of popish intrigue. A controversial exchange in one of the many pamphlets of the crusty Tory apologist Sir Roger L'Estrange makes this widespread distrust and suspicion clear. When Citt, a citizen of London, asks Bumpkin, his country acquaintance, what country folks are discussing over their pots of ale, the latter replies,

... they talk as other people do, of the Plot, and the Jesuits, and the French King, and so.[12]

The three topics were closely interrelated.

Jane Lane, the author of a modern study of Titus Oates and his career, suggests the extent of anti-Catholic feeling when she reminds us that men as sophisticated as John Evelyn and Samuel Pepys "reveal in their diaries how readily they accepted the more fantastic rumours of Popish misdeeds."[13] The tangled events surrounding Oates's astounding "discovery" of a plot to murder the king grew out of the fear of imminent Catholic domination following the Duke of York's second marriage to the Catholic Mary of Modena. A fierce struggle arose in the kingdom, with the king and his brother York on one side, and the Earl of Shaftesbury and the king's natural son, the Duke of Monmouth, on the other. Dryden relates in *Absalom and Achitophel* how the personable Monmouth, eldest of Charles's illegitimate sons, whose mother, Lucy Walters, was the daughter of an impoverished Welsh squire, became a tool of the strong-willed and perfidious Shaftesbury:

> That false Achitophel's pernicious hate
> Had turn'd the Plot to ruin Church and State.[14]
>
> (ll. 929–30)

A popular soldier and successful commander-in-chief, Monmouth was set up by the Whigs as the rival claimant to the throne.

As for the king, even though he had arranged for the marriage of his daughter Mary to the Protestant William of Orange, a union that ultimately kept the monarchy Protestant and limited in its powers, he never wavered in his adherence to the legitimate line of succession. Despite his genuine love for Monmouth, he allowed himself to be persuaded to exile him, as indeed he exiled his brother York for a time. The struggle between the Crown and Parliament was fierce. As G. W. Keeton, one of the historians of the Popish Plot, remarks,

This was, above all others in English history, the age of plots, of informers, and of a despicable breed of adventurers who traded upon the malice or credulity of both factions.[15]

Certainly, the one event that inspired a deluge of lampoons and satires, and helped change the course of English history, was Oates's stunning disclosure to the London Justice of the Peace Sir Edmund Berry Godfrey of a horrid Popish Plot on the life of the King. This "event" was reported as follows in the *Brief Historical Relation of State Affairs* by Narcissus Luttrell (1657–1732), a lawyer, antiquary, and fanatical anti-papist who swallowed Oates's horrifying story whole:

> About the latter end of this month [September, 1678] was a hellish conspiracy, contrived and carried on by the papists, discovered by one Titus Oates unto Sir Edmund Berry Godfrey, justice of the peace, who took his examination on oath.[16]

Oates's disclosures triggered the most bitter partisanship. The Tory view of the whole affair was, perhaps, best expressed by the Duke of York himself, whose eventual accession to the throne was the reason for most of the furor in political circles:

> As for news, this pretended plot is still under examination, and the judges are to give their opinion whether one witness in point of treason be sufficient to proceed criminously against anybody; and I do verily believe that when the affair is thoroughly examined it will find nothing but malice against the poor Catholics in general and myself in particular.[17]

Another contemporary, the Tory historian Roger North, referred to Oates in his *Examen* (1740) as a "dextrous operator," a tool of the Whig Shaftesbury. One of the verses that appeared, in a group of Tory poems inspired by the Plot entitled "A Collection of 86 Loyal Poems" (1685), commented ironically that Oates

> Declares unheard of things before,
> And thousand mysteries doth unfold
> As plain as Oracle of old;
> By which we steer affairs of state
> And stave off Britain's sudden fate.

In any event, on September 6, 1678, Oates appeared before Sir Edmund Berry Godfrey, a highly respected London justice of the peace, not known to hold anti-Catholic views. Three weeks later, he swore a further deposition in the presence of the skeptical and much troubled Godfrey. Shortly thereafter, he was admitted to the Privy Council, where he repeated and further embellished his charges that the Catholics—in particular, the Jesuits—had planned to murder the king so as to bring about the restoration of the old religion.

Popular sentiment against the Catholics reached fever pitch in mid-October when the murdered body of Godfrey, who had been missing from his home for four or five days, was found in a ditch outside London. All of London was aghast. There were even reports of signs and portents on earth and in the heavens. The credulous Luttrell made this entry in his history several months later:

Feb., 1678–9
About the middle of this month, on a Sunday, about eleven in the morning, a prodigious darknesse overspread the face of the sky, the like never known, and continued about half an hour. The darknesse was so great, that in several churches, they could not proceed in divine services without candles; and 'tis said during that time the figure of Sir Edmondbury Godfrey appeared in the queen's chapell at Somerset house while masse was saying.

Oates's sensational revelations, Shaftesbury's shrewdness in fanning the flames of public indignation, the subsequent judicial murders of innocent people, the wild chain of events which continued on into the 1680s—all split further a nation dangerously divided along lines of religious and political allegiance. In *Absalom and Achitophel* Dryden describes the Plot accurately as

> . . . that nation's curse,
> Bad in itself, but represented worse,
> Rais'd in extremes, and in extremes decri'd,
> With oaths affirmed, with dying vows deni'd.
> Not weigh'd or winnow'd by the multitude;
> But swallow'd in the mass, unchew'd and crude,
> Some truth there was, but dash'd and brew'd with lies,
> To please the fools, and puzzle all the wise.
>
> (ll. 108–15)

These splendid lines, besides standing as models of rhetorical balance and antithesis, sum up well the atmosphere of near-hysteria surrounding the Plot.

Oates and His Disclosures

Before a modern reader can place in proper perspective Oldham's vehement attack on the Jesuits and the Catholics, he must have some detailed knowledge of the Plot and its impact on the nation. Therefore, before turning our attention to the *Satires Upon the Jesuits*, we must review the principals and the events.

Oates and a confederate, a pathologically anti-Catholic clergyman named Israel Tonge, unfolded a horrendous tale of a plot by Jesuits to murder the king, massacre honest Protestants, and turn the throne over to James, the Duke of York, who would rule with the aid of a Jesuit clique. Later historians are generally agreed as to the mendacity of Oates. But the whole affair, particularly the never-solved murder of Godfrey, remains perplexing, even in a period so run through with deceit and intrigue—royal, parliamentary, and Jesuitical. That Shaftesbury masterminded a part of the mad affair for his own political ends cannot be doubted. Yet anyone who investigates the Plot with an open mind is left with a conviction that certain highly placed officials of the government were indeed desirous of bringing about a return of the nation to the old religion.

Oates's story was a shocking one. Was it of his own concoction or had it been concocted for him? According to Bishop Burnet, a staunch foe of Roman Catholicism who eventually fell into disfavor with the Stuarts, Charles felt that Oates had been rehearsed in his outlandish tale by Shaftesbury, whom he—the king—wanted confined to the Tower and tried for treason. In his memoirs, Burnet recalls discussing the plot with the king, who

... talked much and very freely with me. We agree in one thing, that the greatest part of the evidence was a contrivance. But he suspected some had set on Oates, and instructed him, and named the Earl of Shaftesbury. I was of another mind. I thought that the many gross things in the narrative showed no abler head than Oates or Tonge in the framing of it....[18]

It is understandable that someone like Burnet, despite his Whig leanings, would dismiss Oates's tale out of hand as a tissue of lies and distortions. Oates's background was a particularly sordid one, hardly one to inspire confidence in him as a witness. The son of a clergyman, who had been dismissed from a regimental chaplaincy by General Monck for encouraging sedition, and afterward expelled from yet another ecclesiastical living, Titus was born in 1649. His school career was undistinguished. But despite having been expelled from the Merchants' Taylor School in 1665, he managed somehow to land at Cambridge University. The account of him in the *Dictionary of National Biography* (XIV) records that one of his tutors at Cambridge left a note, still preserved, in which he called his pupil "a great dunce." By hook or crook, nonetheless, Oates took orders in the Established Church, whereupon he was assigned to a vicarage in Kent. Later he joined his father at All Saints, Hastings.

From this time until his emergence as one of history's greatest conspirators, Oates seems to have plunged himself into one disreputable incident after another. On one occasion he was arrested on an action for a thousand pounds, charged with having, in collaboration with his father, trumped up an accusation against a schoolmaster. He was sent to jail in Dover, where he was to stand trial for perjury. Escaping confinement, he fled to London, and shipped out as a navy chaplain. But he was soon discharged from the naval service because of an apparently ungovernable inclination toward sodomy.

His interest in Rome must have been sparked when he eventually entered service as a chaplain in the household of the Duke of Norfolk, one of the great Roman Catholic establishments of the kingdom, where there was a constant coming and going of priests and adherents of the old faith. At this time, too, he also met Israel Tonge, an eccentric clergyman who busied himself composing attacks on the Jesuits, whom he accused of planning an English St. Bartholomew's Day massacre.

Tonge took on Oates as his literary assistant. Their literary productions, however, attracted, and deserved, little attention. The public neglect of his mentor, presumably, moved Oates to come to his aid through some decisive action. He, therefore, decided to worm his way into the confidence of Catholics. Accordingly, in 1677 he converted to the Church of Rome and thereupon made the acquaintance of certain Jesuits at Somerset House, where the king's Catholic queen had her chapel. Invited to join the order of Ignatius, he went off to the English Jesuit College at Valladolid in Spain. As was customary with him, however, his leanings toward unsavory conduct led to early expulsion. Nonetheless, he claimed to have been awarded the degree of Doctor of Divinity from the University of Salamanca, a claim later proved to be fraudulent.

His brief career as a novice having been of little help in getting first-hand information of Jesuit plotting to Tonge, the tireless Oates

managed to gain admittance to the English Roman Catholic sem-
inary at St. Omer on the Continent. No sooner had he been expelled
for gross misbehavior than he was back in England once more.
It was then that he and Tonge began brewing the details of the
Popish Plot, with the help of one Christopher Kirky, a chemist whose
experiments had brought him to the attention of the king. As a
matter of fact, it was Kirky who first announced to Charles the plot
on his life as the skeptical monarch walked in St. James's Park.

As already indicated, in September, 1678, the affair came to the
ears of the ill-fated Godfrey. Oates's original narrative as presented
to the magistrate contained forty-three articles. Within three weeks
his lively imagination had enlarged the number to eighty-one. The
gist of the charges was that there were no fewer than three schemes
afoot to assassinate the king: first, the king's physician, a Catholic,
had been paid to poison his royal master; second, four Irish thugs
had been employed to stab the king; third, the Jesuits Grove and
Pickering were to be paid fifteen hundred pounds to kill the king
with silver bullets. All this, Oates avowed, had been agreed upon
on April 24, 1678, at a Jesuit provincial consultation held at the
White Horse Tavern in Fleet Street. Once noised abroad, these allegations and the subsequent murder of Godfrey worked the London mob
into a frenzy.

Overnight Oates became a celebrity and popular hero, the high
point of his career arriving when Parliament used his allegations to
embarrass the king and the Duke of York. In October, 1678, he
even appeared before the House of Commons and stated, as the DNB
article on him reports, that

there is and hath been a damnable plot contriv'd and carried on by Popish
recusants for assassinating and murdering the King, for subverting the
government and rooting out and destroying the Protestant religion.

The next year the House ordered that Oates's *True Narrative* be
published.

The wild charges set off a judicial bloodbath. Several other opportunists quickly appeared to confirm Oates's charges. Bishop Burnet
recalls in his memoirs the horrifying execution of Jesuits which the
mischief inspired. He writes: "It was like a letting blood, (as one
observed), which abates a fever."[19] A poem of the time by one John
Caryll (1625–1711) entitled *Naboth's Vineyard* (reprinted in Yale

POAS II) suggests all the madness and horror of the whole episode from the standpoint of the victim of the judicial murders. Himself a member of an old Catholic family and connected to the Duke of York by strong Royalist sympathies, Caryll was a suspect in the Plot and was imprisoned in the Tower in 1679. In his poem, which anticipates *Absalom and Achitophel* in its use of a biblical parallel, he retells the story of how King Ahab coveted the vineyard of Naboth, as related in the first book of Kings. When Naboth steadfastly refuses to part with his land, Queen Jezebel counsels her husband to acquire the property through judicial proceedings. Arod, representing the Lord Chief Justice Sir William Scroggs who played a leading role in prosecuting those accused in the Popish Plot, conveniently locates two "witnesses," Malchus and Python. These two correspond to Oates and William Bedloe (who avowed that the former had made his disclosures in anticipation of his own). In the story as told in Kings, both swear before the tribes of Israel on the high holy days that Naboth has blasphemed God and the king. Speaking in his own defense before he is rushed out to be killed by the outraged people, Naboth expresses eloquently what must have been the feelings of those unfortunates accused of complicity in the Popish Plot:

> These vipers in the bosom of our law
> Will eat it through, its very heartstrings gnaw;
> For when with artificial perjury
> They make God's sacred Name espouse their lie,
> Forthwith that lie omnipotent becomes
> And governs all below—it saves or dooms....
>
> (ll. 398–402)

It falls to Queen Jezebel, early in the poem, to voice the principle on which demagogues and agitators in all ages proceed:

> In great designs it is the greatest art
> To make the common people take your part.
> Some words there are which have a special charm
> To wind their fancies up to an alarm:
> Treason, Religion, Liberty are such;
> Like clocks they strike when on those points you touch.
>
> (ll. 163–68)

The skepticism of the king himself and more sophisticated contemporaries never weakened. But for the ordinary Englishman, the

Plot seemed monstrous beyond all imagining, so vile, indeed, as to make Oldham's Jesuits, whom he portrays in the *Satires Upon the Jesuits* as very monsters of depravity, seem perfectly credible. What lay before the Houses of Parliament, in the words of a contemporary account, was

...no less than the murder of the king, the subversion of our religion, laws and properties, the introducing of popery and a tyrannical arbitrary government....[20]

As already noted, Oates told his story repeatedly, modifying and embroidering details at will. A genuinely unpleasant character, physically repugnant and addicted to sodomy, he was reviled as much as he was defended—

'Tis Oates, bare Oates, which is become
The health of England, bane of Rome . . .
Nay, to add to the wonder more
Declares unheard-of things before.[21]

The already-mentioned anti-Catholic lawyer and antiquary Narcissus Luttrell, who never wavered in his faith in Oates, kept a list of publications inspired by the Plot, publishing it anonymously in 1680 and 1681 under the long title, *A Complete Catalogue of All the Stich'd Books and Single Sheets, Printed since the First Discovery of the Popish Plot.* The period covered extends from September, 1678 to June, 1680. The list shows that during those months the Plot and related topics formed the subject of close to one hundred pamphlets, sermons, and verse pieces. Luttrell's annotations indicate his complete acceptance of Oates's veracity and his steadfast belief in a Catholic conspiracy.[22]

As noted, most historians have dismissed Oates as an out-and-out liar. Sir John Dalyrymple, a politician and memoirist of the succeeding century, declared that Shaftesbury

framed the fiction of the Popish Plot in order to bring the Duke [York], and perhaps the King, under the weight of the national fear and hatred of Popery.[23]

A contemporary observer, J. G. Muddiman, a recorder of parliamentary events known to later ages as the "King's Journalist," asserted that the nation finally came to the realization, thanks to the king and the efforts of Roger L'Estrange, that the Plot was a hoax perpetrated by Shaftesbury and the Whigs to exclude the Catholic James II from the royal succession—which indeed Shaftesbury tried to accomplish through an act of Parliament that was thwarted only by the Lords.[24] Yet certain unexplained circumstances, notably the mysterious murder of Godfrey, lend a modicum of substance to Oates's charges. In the present century, the lawyer and historian Sir John Pollock has maintained that figures like Edward Coleman, the Duke of York's secretary who was condemned to death as a conspirator, probably did have designs of restoring England to the Roman fold, but without violence to the person of the king. Pollock is well aware that Shaftesbury turned the murder of Godfrey and the narrative of Oates to his own political advantage. Still—and it must be noted that his view is a minority one—he argues that so much smoke must have contained some fire:

Oates was not after all aiming shafts entirely at random. During his stay in the Jesuit seminaries in Spain and Flanders he must have obtained an inkling of what was in the air, and proceeded to act upon the information to his best advantage. That the whole truth had little resemblance to his tale of fire and massacre is certain, but the tale was not wholly devoid of truth. His vast superstructure of lies was not without a slight basis of solid fact.[25]

Just how much fire there was has not been determined. But Oates laid down a thick smoke screen before he was eventually disgraced, flogged, and committed to prison for several years in 1685 as a perjuror—but not before he had been responsible for sending about thirty-five innocent people to their death. It is an understatement to say that the charges he and Tonge concocted had impressive results. As the present-day historian Maurice Ashley reminds us, their narrative

resulted in the judicial murders of Jesuits and Catholics, forced the Duke of York into exile, destroyed the Cavalier Parliament, raised the Earl of Shaftesbury, as opposition leader, to the pinnacle of power, created the party system and imperilled the throne itself.[26]

Any reader interested in savoring the excitement and air of fear and distrust engendered by the horrid plot need only turn to the Yale

POAS II, wherein he can read, among other warnings, this one to Englishmen spoken by the ghost of the murdered Godfrey in "Sir Edmund Berry Godfrey's Ghost" (1679):

> Repent in time, and banish from your sight
> The pimp, the whore, buffoon, Church parasite.

This intense suspicion and horror of the Pope and his henchmen form the backdrop of Oldham's *Satires Upon the Jesuits.* To the modern reader lacking in appreciation of what the Plot meant to the ordinary Englishman of the time, who saw in a Protestant monarchy the only chance for political stability and freedom from Continental intrigue, Oldham's satires can seem little more than the ranting associated with the impossible figures of the seventeenth-century heroic drama. But the exaggerated dread of Rome was genuine. As already indicated, we need only turn to the volumes of *POAS* for abundant confirmation. The following lines, attributed to the hapless Stephen College, must have reflected the view of many ordinary Englishmen of Oldham's and Oates's time:

> The best of men by wretched means they kill,
> To serve their Church and gain their cursed will.
> Say but Rome's vicar, "Such a man must die,"
> That's crime enough, no matter how or why.[27]

Satires Upon the Jesuits

Composition.   By a lucky chance, in a period that has left scholars so many problems of attribution, there is no question about the authorship of the *Satires Upon the Jesuits.* The already discussed Bodleian manuscript notebook in Oldham's own hand contains early versions of the satires and marginal revisions. The unfolding of the Plot in 1678 and 1679 presented Oldham with the kind of opportunity he had the talent to exploit. As Brooks says, with the still unsolved murder of the London magistrate to whom Titus Oates disclosed the Popish Plot, and with the full horror seizing upon both Tories and Whigs,

Oldham determined to satirize the Jesuits, believed to be the arch-champions of Counter-Reformation.[28]

The first satire of the series was printed as a broadside in 1679, without the author's consent. An authorized edition of the entire series of four appeared in 1681, while the furor was still raging. Oldham himself, in an advertisement contained in his manuscript notebook but never published, complained of the inaccuracies of the pirated edition:

One of the [*Satires Upon the Jesuits*] was lately printed without his knowledge of the straggling copies that passed about the town, which besides the uncorrectness it went with from his hands, was so miserably mangled and abused by the ignorance and mistakes of transcribers that 'twas now become a greater satire on himself than those upon whom it was written.

Brooks's *Bibliography* lists editions of the satires that appeared well into the eighteenth century, during which century interest in them waned. Once readers' taste for Juvenalian vigor of language and attack had been refined by the gentler and more urbane Horatian mode, and once the memory of the Plot had dimmed, interest in the satires declined. The only text easily available to modern students is that in the nineteenth-century bowdlerized edition of Oldham's works by Robert Bell. H. F. Brooks, who has already been cited frequently, promises us a careful edition of the complete works, which he reports a publisher has accepted in principle.

Fortunately for students of today, Yale *POAS* II, ably edited by Elias F. Mengel, Jr., contains a well-annotated edition of the *Satires Upon the Jesuits*, with the text of the first satire, often called "Garnett's Ghost," based upon a careful collation of the first three editions and pirated broadsides versions. The Yale press and the general editor of *POAS* have rendered a valuable service to seventeenth-century scholarship by including the entire series of satires in the second volume. Professor Mengel renders a further service by including in the same volume a well-annotated text of *Absalom and Achitophel*, thereby encouraging readers to compare Dryden's masterful achievement with Oldham's now largely neglected anti-Catholic satire.

A reviewer in the *Times Literary Supplement* of November 25, 1965, expressed hope that the publication of Yale *POAS* II might lead to a revaluation of Oldham. As he notes, after *Absalom*

the finest poems in the volume in question are without doubt Oldham's
Satires Upon the Jesuits, which at times have an authentic Juvenalian
flavor.

He goes on to say that after reading these satires with the attention
they deserve, the reader can recognize the justice of Dryden's tribute
in the moving elegy on his "too little and too lately known" young
friend. With justice, Yale editor Mengel concludes his introductory
note to the text with this statement:

The long tradition of English anti-Catholic satire, Juvenalian in its savage-
ness and particularly directed at the Jesuits, culminates in Oldham's attack.

The Prologue to the Satires.   In the manner of Roman satire,
the prologue to the *Satires Upon the Jesuits* presents the *raison d'être*,
or the occasion of the work. It was a convention during the Restoration for writers to think of themselves as gentlemen dabbling in or
drawn, beyond their powers to control themselves, to the somewhat
low profession of letters by a need to castigate manners and morals.
With the examples of Persius and Juvenal before him, Oldham announces that he cannot refrain from entering the lists against those
who would subvert the established order and undermine king and
religion. Juvenal began his celebrated and much-imitated first satire
with the exasperated question of a long-suffering man who no longer
can stomach the abuses he sees everywhere about him. Must I be
nothing more than a listener, the Roman asked, and never strike
back? (*Semper ego auditor tantum? Numquamne reponam?*) Oldham
manages an equally blunt opening, a first-rate adaptation of Juvenal's
opening lines:

> For who can longer hold? when ev'ry press,
> The bar and pulpit too, has broke the peace?
> When ev'ry scribbling fool at the alarms
> Has drawn his pen, and rises up in arms?
> And not a dull pretender of the town
> But vents his gall in pamphlet up and down?
> When all with license rail, and who will not
> Must be almost suspected of the Plot. . . .

Such vigorous lines, of course, found inspiration in more than the
conventional desire to echo the Roman satirists in an age when most

readers were on at least speaking terms with the Latin classics. As the lines themselves state, and as we know from a source such as Luttrell's catalog, the Plot had prompted effusions of many kinds. Oldham had indeed been presented with an authentic Juvenalian occasion in that he saw in the machinations of the Catholics a real threat to country and religion. Ordinary preachers and divines, he argues, were hardly a match for the cunning and devious followers of Loyola—

> In vain our preaching tribe attack the foes,
> In vain their weak artillery oppose:
>
> .   .   .
>
> Would they the dull old fisherman compare
> With mighty Suarez and great Escobar?

The two Jesuits named were masters of Scholastic subtlety and casuistry. It was Suarez (1548–1617) who, encouraged by Pope Paul V, wrote the treatise, *Defensio Catholicae fidei contra Anglicanae sectae errores*, in which he singled out and attacked Anglican "errors" of faith, censuring especially the Oath of Allegiance James I had required of all Englishmen. What chance can "mistaken honest men" who preach "gentle doctrine" have against such foes?

> 'Tis pointed satire and the sharps of wit
> For such a prize are th' only weapons fit.

Once again echoing his literary model Juvenal, who informed his Roman readers that indignation rather than natural inclination made him write (*si natura negat, facit indignatio versum*), Oldham suggests the magnitude of the evil that forces him to write:

> Nor needs there art or genius here to use,
> Where indignation can create a muse.

As a satirist, it is his sacred duty to avenge the murdered Godfrey and all Englishmen threatened and injured by the "vile brood of Loyola"—

> It is resolv'd: henceforth an endless war
> I and my Muse with them and theirs declare.

His weapon in this war is "a stabbing pen"; his motive, retribution:

> Red hot with vengeance thus, I'll brand disgrace
> So deep no time shall e'er the marks deface.

He warns that Jesuits and all in league with them can expect no quarter. With the hyperbole that marks the larger-than-life protagonists of the contemporary heroic plays, Oldham vows never to "cease to persecute and plague their cursed race."

He more than lives up to his promise. In the satires that follow he heaps abuse on his enemies in vigorous rhythms and rough rhymes. A reader must prepare himself for cascades of abuse and relentless assault. With faint but unmistakably ironic overtones of Marvell's protestations of undying love in "To His Coy Mistress," he promises:

> Sooner shall false Court favorites prove just
> And faithful to their King's and country's trust;
> Sooner shall they detect the tricks of state,
> And knav'ry, suits, and bribes, and flatt'ry hate;
> Bawds shall turn nuns, salt duchesses grown chaste,
> And paint and pride and lechery detest;
> Pope's shall for kings' supremacy decide,
> And cardinals for Huguenots be tried;
> Sooner (which is the great'st impossible)
> Shall the vile brood of Loyola and Hell
> Give o'er to plot, be villains, and rebel
> Than I with utmost spite and vengeance cease
> To persecute and plague their cursed race.

Satire I: Garnett's Ghost

Once we have tried as best we can to put ourselves in the position of readers of Oldham's own time, we can appreciate how skilled a propagandist he was, even though readers in the days of Oates's triumph needed little persuading that the Jesuits and their "hellish brood" were dedicated to the destruction of Englishmen's liberties and the Protestant conscience. In the first satire the ghost of Henry Garnett, the English Jesuit provincial who was cruelly executed in 1606 for his alleged complicity in the Gunpowder Plot the year before, speaks to fellow Jesuits rejoicing and glorying in Godfrey's murder.

Garnett (also Garnet) was born in 1555, eventually went to London to study law, converted to Catholicism somewhere along the line, and went to Italy in 1575 to join the Jesuits. He was named provincial of the English province in 1575. Like fellow Jesuits of the time, he courageously, even recklessly, ministered to the Catholic population and the great recusant families. Among Protestants, however, he came to be associated with the notorious doctrine of equivocation, a position refined and championed by some of the Jesuit moral theologians, in particular. It was this doctrine and his implication in the Gunpowder Plot that led to his eventual undoing. Garnett, it was charged, became aware of the Plot to blow up the Houses of Parliament "by way of confession," but did nothing to prevent it. It was also alleged that he had urged priests to avoid stirring up civil disorders and conspiracy, but not to hinder such actions already underway, if they were likely to promote the Catholic cause. When he was put on trial for his part in the Plot, his detractors and enemies were outraged by his stubborn persistence in equivocating. In Protestant circles, his career was regarded as the epitome of Jesuit duplicity and unceasing plotting to overturn the new order in England.

The memory of the Gunpowder Plot was still fairly recent. Readers of Oldham's time were also well aware that on December 21, 1678, one Miles Prance, a Roman Catholic silversmith who had done some work in the Queen's chapel in Somerset House, had been arrested and charged with having conspired with certain Jesuits in an attempt on the king's life. The charge was based on little more than the trumped-up story of someone to whom Prance owed a sum of money. After unremitting interrogation and cruel torture, the helpless silversmith "confessed" to having aided a group of priests murder the unfortunate magistrate Godfrey because he was a good Protestant and a known foe of the conspiracies to return England to the tyranny of Rome. Many frightened, loyal Englishmen certainly must have believed what the corpse of Godfrey is made to proclaim in an anonymous piece cited earlier, "Sir Edmund Berry Godfrey's Ghost":

> I for religion, rights, and liberties
> Am mangl'd thus, and made a sacrifice.

The unknown author of another Whig satire included in the Yale *POAS* II, "Popish Politics Unmasked" (1680), also plays upon genuine fears when he has the Duke of York advise his brother the king as follows:

> ... laws are nothing else but ties and bands
> On purpose made to shackle subjects' hands.

The bloody declamations of Garnett in the first satire, outrageously exaggerated as they may seem to a modern reader unacquainted with the ferocious anti-Catholic sentiment of the time, surely found receptive ears in Oldham's own time.

In having Garnett fulminate the way he does, Oldham was doing more than adapt the rant of the heroic drama to his purposes. He was following the example of one of his models, Ben Jonson, in whose play *Catiline* the ghost of Sylla (Sulla) appears to declaim and advocate the destruction of the Roman republic. The martyred Jesuit is addressing a meeting of fellows convened in celebration of Godfrey's death. (The weak and infamous Prance testified that he had indeed attended such a victory party called by Jesuits and other priests.) He revels in the murder and makes no attempt to conceal the perfidy of his order. After all, he is surrounded by his fellows from whom there is no need of concealment. Godfrey's killing was "bravely done"—

> So fare all they who e'er provoke our hate.

A satanic figure, whose ravings at times remind one of Milton's Lucifer who chose to reign in hell rather than serve in Heaven, he will not adore "the purple rag of majesty," and urges his followers to cast off all qualms and honor everything opposed to true religion. By so doing, he tells them,

> ... you're true Jesuits, then you're fit to be
> Disciples of great Loyola and me.
> Worthy to undertake, worthy a Plot
> Like this, and fit to scourge an Huguenot.

Garnett, a stage villain, flings his hair-raising curses with wild abandon at everything the Protestant Englishman of Oldham's time held dear. He reviles Queen Elizabeth, "a late reigning witch," and Luther, "that apostate monk." He singles out for praise whatever the trueborn Protestant is taught to abhor—for example, Rome's pursuit of heretics and ruthless suppression of heresy:

> Too sparing was the time, too mild the day,
> When our great Mary bore the English sway;
>
> .   .   .
>
> Had I had the pow'r
> Or been thought fit t' have been her counselor,
>
> .   .   .
>
> Big bonfires should have blaz'd and shone each day
> To tell our triumphs, and make bright our way.

To inflame his readers even more, Oldham has Garnett urge his followers to emulate the glorious slaughter of the Huguenots which had occurred in France on St. Bartholomew's Day in 1572. (Many of his contemporary readers were surely acquainted with descendants of these French Protestants who had fled to England for safety during the bloodbath.) Garnett brings matters to a thundering climax with horrifying praise of Charles IX, who acting on the urgings of his Italian mother, Catherine De Medici, had ordered the massacre of the Huguenots—

> How goodly was the sight: how fine the show!
> When Paris saw through all its channels flow
> The blood of Huguenots; when the full Seine,
> Swell'd with the flood, its banks with joy o'erran!

Such lines held real terror for readers who had been shocked and outraged by the disclosures of Titus Oates and the testimony of Prance and others:

> This [the massacre of the Huguenots] a king did—
> and great and mighty 'twas—
> Worthy his high degree and pow'r and place,
> And worthy our religion and our cause.

Recounting the "noble" deeds of an earlier French king was, no doubt, intended to hold warning for an English king skeptical of the revelations of popish plotting, as well as a warning to the subjects of the same king whose own leanings were unmistakably Romish and whose designated successor was an avowed adherent of the old religion. Garnett and his Jesuits represent everything abhorrent to a Protestantism endangered by the Catholicizing tendencies of the Stuarts. These followers of Loyola are painted by Oldham as truly devilish figures, never daunted by

> That hated Book, the bulwark of our foes.

Instead, they

> ... have only will
> Like fiends ... to covet and act ill.

Garnett's frenzy increases melodramatically as the satire progresses. He urges his Catholic followers to surpass the ancient pagan Catiline in crime, the speech even echoing lines from the first act of Jonson's play:

> Kill like a plague or inquisition: spare
> No age, degree, or sex; only to wear
> A soul, only to own a life, be here
> Thought crime enough to lose't. ...

Delay no longer, he commands his followers, but begin to burn the city, destroy all who are investigating the Catholic conspiracy—spare no one. And, a command carefully calculated to chill a loyal English heart: destroy England herself, a feat more than "Spain or Eighty-Eight could e'er devise."

Such lines speak for themselves. This is bombast designed to inflame contemporary readers and transform mere allegations of plotting into a series of already committed atrocities.

The first satire demonstrates that Oldham possessed the gifts of the master propagandist. But to appreciate his skill, a serious modern reader must try to place himself in the position of a reader of 1680, with his memories of the Spanish threat of 1588, Guy Fawkes and the Gunpowder Plot, Bloody Mary and the Protestant martyrs, and his certainty that bands of villainous Jesuits and Catholics were intent on destroying hard-won English liberties and the Protestant conscience. Garnett sums matters up frighteningly when he reminds his followers:

What neither Saxon rage could here inflict,
Nor Danes more savage, nor the barb'rous Pict;
What Spain or Eighty-Eight could e'er devise,
With all its fleet and freight of cruelties;
What ne'er Medina wish'd, much less could dare,
And Bloodier Alva would with trembling hear:
What may strike out dire prodigies of old,
And make their mild and gentler acts untold;
What Heaven's judgments, nor the angry stars,
Foreign invasion, nor domestic wars,
Plague, fire nor famine could effect or do—
All this and more be dar'd and done by you.

Satire II

In the second of the satires the poet speaks out in his own voice, guided, as he tells his readers in an Advertisement, by "the swing of his own genius." In his role as fiery preacher, he prays Heaven to bring down upon the nation any punishment milder than the plague that now infects it—anything

To have this worst of ills remov'd away.

By giving birth to Loyola, "Proud Spain" has more than avenged herself for the loss of her Armada in '88 and the national humiliation she suffered at the hands of Drake and gallant English crews.

But all this is merely preliminary skirmishing. The poet now turns to a frontal attack on Loyola, the instrument of Spain's vengeance—

Great counter plague! in which unhappy we
Pay back her suff'rings with full usury.

Unfortunately, as is too often the case with him, Oldham is least effective when he goes on the direct attack. His venom and sheer abusiveness repel a reader who cannot accept the object of the assault as the sum total of all evil. He curses, for example, the shell that maimed the youthful Loyola when he was soldier for Spain, because it failed to kill him—

More curst that ill-aim'd shot which basely miss'd,
Which maim'd a limb, but spar'd thy hated breast,
And made thee't once a cripple and a priest.

Even the ending of the last line quoted, as clever a use of the rhetorical figure called syllepsis as it is, must have appalled some stalwart Protestant readers. He is much more effective when he employs irony and indirection, as when, for example, he withdraws his curse and reflects ironically that without Loyola and his Jesuits,

> The Church ... might lack
> Champions, good works, and saints for th' almanac,

and the "Roman sultan" might lack "janizaries of the cause." Then, cleverly playing on the Protestant Englishman's abhorrence of Spain and Catholic practices—after all, the Armada and the martyrs of Bloody Mary's reign were only a century in the past—he goes on to remind readers that without the Jesuits, Spain could not have made her great contribution to the New World. After all, the Spaniards are the ones

> ... by whose means both Indies now enjoy
> The two choice blessings, pox and Popery.

It is easy, continues Oldham, to see why Loyola traded his soldier's armor for the Jesuit's soutane. After all, have not the Jesuits' forays into the New World been every bit as ruthless as those of the Spanish conquistadores? The Jesuit also has an important advantage, his casuistry, the art of devising a justification for any and every act of cruelty. He is, as the poet says in an apparent reference to the murder of the hapless Godfrey,

> Your cool and sober murderer, who prays
> And stabs at the same time....

This second satire is a free-flowing denunciation, and the thought of Jesuitical cruelty launches the poet on a vehement anti-Catholic tirade, in the course of which he serves up all the stock charges against the sons of Loyola, in particular their shocking tactic of making ends justify means—

> The blackest, ugliest, horridst, damnedst deed,
>   .   .   .
> If done for Holy Church is sanctifi'd.

If anyone be abhorred by ordinary, decent men as a villain, let him be revered by me, says the Jesuit:

> Rebellion, treason, murder, massacre
> The chief ingredients now of saintship are.

Oldham must speak out once more in his own voice, and, over-whelmed at the thought of Jesuit infamy, calls upon the Lord to smite His enemies in the tones of a prophet of the Old Testament.

Interestingly enough, and unfortunately for the poet, in the last section of this satire the speaker risks turning the argument against himself by arousing sympathy for martyred Jesuits. They perish in their perfidy, even when they are hunted down and caught and put to the supreme test—

> ... glorious and heroic constancy
> That can forswear upon the cart, and die
> With gasping souls expiring in a lie.

This is almost an inadvertent expression of grudging admiration, even though their constancy is not due to a love of virtue, but rests on equivocation and firm allegiance to "Hell's Prince."

As for equivocation, with the memory of Garnett's evasions and deceptions still alive, the speaker has solemn words of warning for kings, for example, Charles and his brother York, who place their trust in Jesuits:

> ... who with more ease
> Can swallow down most solemn perjuries
> Than a town bully common oaths and lies.

As the satire reaches its conclusion—it runs for some two hundred and eighty-five lines—the modern reader can easily lose patience with what turns into unbridled rant. The speaker calls on the English to extirpate the Jesuit menace, and place a bounty on them as bounties were used to rid England of wolves in earlier times. The hyperbole is typical of Oldham. Too often it is blown completely out of all proportion. The overall tone, that of Old Testament prophet and preacher inflamed by a just anger, grates on readers' ears nowadays. Still, there are glimpses of a genuine poetic talent at work, particu-

larly when Oldham is imitating others. These lines, for example, have
a majestic ring suggestive of Milton's sonnet "On the Late Massacre
in Piedmont":

> Hearst thou, great God, such daring blasphemy,
> And letst thy patient thunder still lie by?
> Strike and avenge, lest impious atheists say
> Chance guides the world and has usurp'd thy sway.

Or, he manages to capture the sardonic flavor of Donne's hyperbole
in a poem like "Go and catch a falling star"—

> Think Tories loyal, or Scotch Cov'nanters;
> Robb'd tigers gentle; courteous, fasting bears;
> Atheists devout, and thrice-wrack'd mariners;
> Take goats for chaste, and cloister'd marmosites;
> For plain and open, two-edg'd parasites;
> Believe bawds modest, and the shameless stews;
> And binding drunkards' oaths, and strumpets' vows;
> And when in time these contradictions meet,
> Then hope to find 'em in a Loyolite:
> To whom, though gasping, should I credit give,
> I'd think't were sin, and damn'd like unbelief.

In brief, so goes the argument of the second satire, there is no
creature more perfidious than a Jesuit, of whom the archetype is the
Spaniard Loyola. Even when dead, they are villainous. Loyal Englishmen have no choice but to rid the island of them, and

> . . . let their mangl'd quarters hang the isle
> To scare all future vermin from the soil.

Satire III: Loyola's Will

Longest of the series, running over six hundred lines, this satire is
modeled on a Latin poem by George Buchanan attacking the Franciscans, *Franciscanus*, published in 1560. This attack by Buchanan
(1506–1582), which had the encouragement of the Scottish King,
James V, helped further the cause of the Reformation in Scotland.
The speaker in the Latin original is a former friar. As such, he is in
a position to reveal the cunning and lechery of his former fellows

and describe how they bilk simpleminded rustics. Rather than a manual of piety, the poem is a manual of knavery and deceit. Since the speaker discloses his own villainy, the disclosures have some of the bite of Chaucer's *Pardoner's Tale*, in which an earlier clerical knave reveals his own knavery and the tricks he plays on the credulous.

Who are the people who become Franciscans, the speaker asks. A gallery of rogues is the answer. After serving his novitiate in deceptive bearing and speech, a novice is apprenticed to an older friar who shows him how to make fools of the credulous and live a life of luxury and vice. The most important tool of his profession, the friar learns, is the confessional. The best place to practice knavery is the countryside, where people are more gullible. One lesson the aspiring Franciscan must learn early is to avoid the teachings of St. Paul, the apostle who taught that man is justified by faith.

The speaker in Oldham's satire is the founder of the Jesuits, Loyola himself, who has summoned his disciples to his deathbed. In a scene somewhat reminiscent of Pandemonium in Book I of *Paradise Lost* ("On pillow rais'd, he doest their entrance greet"), the dying leader addresses his fallen ones. He is like Lucifer in that the loyal Protestant reader, convinced of Jesuit villainy, knows that he will be sent to the very depths of hell once he is dead. Fellow Jesuits swarm around him as the fallen angels swarmed around their leader. Oldham provides a generous helping of the disgusting details with which he was fond of larding his satire. Whenever Loyola speaks, for example,

> ...from his mouth long flakes of drivel flow.

Aware that his time is running out, his eloquence mounts as he harangues his followers to carry on the work of the Counter-Reformation, remain faithful to the Pope ("our great Caliph"), and stamp out heresy. In lines designed to inflame loyal Protestant readers against both the Jesuits and the Tory supporters of the Duke of York, he calls for the return of England to the Roman fold:

> Make stubborn England once more stoop its crown,
> And fealty to our priestly sov'reign own.

Protestantism must be driven out, and the island cleared of "all remaining dregs of Wyclif there."

Loyola expresses regret that he will not live to see his followers
conquer England for Rome once again. Like an heroic general dying
in battle and surrounded by his loyal staff, he issues his final orders.
First, he admonishes his companions to remain faithful to their
Jesuit oath and to the Pope, whose legions they are. Oldham then
puts into his mouth all the doctrines that for Protestants of the time
were the targets of their arguments against papistry. These doctrines
seem especially shocking since we are hearing them from the inside,
so to speak. For example, no matter how unpleasant the Pope may
be, says Loyola, whether he be

> . . . pander, bawd, pimp, pathic, buggerer,

he deserves blind, unquestioning obedience. (A "pathic" is a man or
a boy on whom sodomy is practiced.) Loyola reminds his Jesuits that
they are to defy reason and nature itself in their devotion to the
Pope and Romanism:

> Forswear your reason, conscience, and your creed,
> Your very sense, and Euclid if he bid.

His second charge has to do with those who are recruited for the
Jesuit order. It shows him to be a master psychologist. First, recruit
above all others, he urges, those who desert the enemy. Second, stay
on the lookout always for the learned and tempt their vanity "with
hopes of honors, scarlet gowns. . . ." Finally, with heavy-handed irony,
he warns them never to rule out the discontented or candidates whose
only failing is that of moral turpitude—

> So Rome's and Mecca's first great founders did,
> By such wise methods made their churches spread.

All recruits, he commands, are to be trained "to a well-bred shame-
lessness." Above all, make sure that they develop that one characteristic which their enemies are agreed is the mark of the true Jesuit—

> that great gift and talent, impudence,
> Accomplished mankind's highest excellence.

Playing cleverly on the fears and biases of his readers, Oldham
has Loyola dismiss religion as a genuine element in the Jesuit's

life. It is enough, he counsels, to cultivate the outward forms of religion only. As a guiding principle, be careful not to admit the "nice, holy conscientious ass" to Jesuit society. The Jesuit is a Machiavel, whose prime concern is "interest." There is also no need, the dying leader exhorts, for austerity. Leave that to others and

> Live you in luxury and pamper'd ease.

The gentle Nazarene is not a fit model for a Jesuit; a more appropriate model is Iscariot.

In a section in which Oldham follows Buchanan's Latin original closely, Loyola gives careful directions as to how guileless people can be cozened. Locate and strike at the weaknesses of each group, he advises. The great rule, of course, is to play upon the credulity of the common people by feeding them stories of miracles of the Virgin and a miscellany of miraculous occurrences, such marvels as

> How pigs to th' ros'ry kneel'd, and sheep were taught
> To bleat *Te Deum* and *Magnificat*.

As this passage demonstrates, Oldham possessed a talent for piling up repugnant details, the talent that enables him as the satire progresses to expand effectively upon what every true-blue Protestant abhorred as the abuse of the confessional. Where appeals to credulity are concerned, Loyola counsels, Jesuits must not forget confession, "our chief privilege and boast." This it is that gives the Jesuit power over kings, misers, and luscious maids. More important, however, is deciding how a sinner is to atone, once he has been shriven. For the poor, it is enough that they chastise their bodies. For those with money, making pilgrimages, building churches—these are the acts of penance that expiate sin. Remember, Loyola commands,

> A small bequest to th' church can all atone,
> Wipes off all scores, and Heav'n and all's their own.

Above all, see to it, Loyola warns his minions, that all Bibles are kept from the homes of the people—

> Happy the time when th' unpretending crowd
> No more than I its language understood!

From placing Scripture into the hands of the common people have issued all the troubles that beset the Jesuit, the plague of Protestantism, in particular. Oldham cleverly has Loyola confirm the fears of the loyal Protestant and give substance to one of the most common charges against the Catholic clergy in the following lines. How much better it was

> When the worm-eaten book, link'd to a chain,
> In dust lay molding in the Vatican—
> Despis'd, neglected and forgot—
> To none but poring rabbis or the Sorbonne known.

For that matter, religious matters are simple affairs, easy to understand. A wily Jesuit concerns himself with weightier things—for instance, how to depose kings and incite nations to rebellion:

> How bubbl'd monarchs are at first beguil'd,
> Trepann'd and gull'd, at last depos'd and kill'd.

The strategy for this is simple. First of all, the chief Jesuit tells his followers, find a rogue. Then, he continues, bind him by solemn oath. Promise him pardon and riches, and if he should fail in his brave attempts, a reward in Heaven. Instruct him in the subtle Latin art of murder—"worth the genius of a Machiavel." And above all else, impress upon him that if he fail, he must never confess and "shame the church." Rather, he must

> Cog, shame, outface, deny, equivocate.

In short, a Jesuit uses any means to achieve his end, except to tell the truth ("Cog" means to be deceitful.) Contemporary readers at this point must have recalled the murder of Godfrey and the Jesuits and their accomplices who, according to Oates and other informers, were desirous of taking the king's life. Those with longer memories, as well as one who had read the first satire in the series, remembered the earlier Jesuit Garnett and the Gunpowder Plot.

But at length the great leader grows faint. In a stroke sure to strike terror into the heart of the Protestant Englishman, he adjures his followers by his own *Spiritual Exercises* to keep forever secret what he has revealed of Jesuit craft. Those assembled

> ... kneel and all the sacred volume kiss,
> Vowing to send each year an hecatomb,
> Of Huguenots as off'ring to his tomb.

Whereupon, like the accursed Dr. Faustus, Loyola is carried off to the lower regions:

> Amen is echo'd by infernal howl,
> And scrambling spirits seize his parting soul.

As any reader familiar to any degree with the anti-Catholic, anti-Jesuit sermonizing and pamphleteering of the troubled period in England before the accession of William and Mary will recognize, in this satire Oldham exhausts the standard arsenal of charges. These were familiar to contemporary readers: the duplicity of the Catholic clergy, the superstitions of Catholic practices, the Machiavellian character of the Jesuit, the Jesuits' blind adherence to popery. The fact, too, that somewhere beyond the Alps, the Pope was lurking gave Oldham an opportunity to exploit the normal Englishman's traditional distrust of Italy and Italian trickery and deceit. Thus, he plays cleverly upon the whole keyboard of anti-Catholic feeling and bias and makes use of every anti-Catholic canard. Ludicrous though it may strike the twentieth-century reader, the portrait of the Jesuit as a ranting Tamerlane, to whom restoring papistry is the end justified by any means, no matter how foul, must have been chilling indeed to a reader like Narcissus Luttrell and those who shared his convictions. For them the details and horrors of the Popish Plot were the substance of daily conversation, a plot hatched and furthered by those who

> Lay cities, countries, realms, whole Nature waste.
> Sack, ravish, burn, destroy, slay, massacre.

Satire IV

Once again Loyola speaks in the last satire. By again making him the rascally speaker, Oldham gives himself a splendid opportunity to display his considerable gifts for the scatological. This time the chief Jesuit speaks not in his own physical person, but through a statue or image—an image of the saint supposed to be revered by Catholics. This choice of situation, of course, was designed to arouse

in Protestant readers detestation of the Catholic practice of revering
statues and graven images. In addition, as Oldham announces in an
"Advertisement," he took as model for his fourth satire the Eighth
Satire of Horace, wherein Priapus, the god of gardens and fertility
who sports an oversized male appendage, speaks from where he is
enshrined in a cemetery. In Horace's satire the god complains bitterly and noisily of the witches who gather in the graveyard at
night to practice their disgusting rites.

Loyola's image speaks from the church in which it is enshrined.
The satire's opening is a faithful rendering of Horace's opening line,
so well known to Latinists—*Olim truncus eram ficulnus, inutile
lignum.* But the expansion immediately establishes the level of abuse:

> Once I was common wood, a shapeless log,
> Thrown out a pissing-post for ev'ry dog,
> The workman yet in doubt what course to take,
> Whether I'd best a saint or hog-trough make,
> After debate resolv'd me for a saint
> And thus fam'd Loyola I represent;
> And well may I resemble him, for he
>
> .   .   .
>
> As stupid was, as much a block as I.

Piling one revolting detail on another even more revolting, the
talking image describes the superstitions and flummeries of the Roman
religion. He ticks off the Romish practices and beliefs certain to
inflame a Protestant Englishman still shocked by the murder of
Godfrey and the horrors of the plot on the king's life as elaborated
by the infamous Oates and his associates. Loyola calls attention to the
belief the credulous have in the miracles wrought by his image—and
the gifts bestowed upon the Church by the credulous to show their
gratitude. Cynically, he singles out holy sights and objects that de-
ceive the ignorant, for example, priests "like mountebanks on stage"
palming off on the faithful sacred relics and holy oils. Agnostic and
deceiver of the innocent that he is at heart, Loyola even points blas-
phemously to the pyx in which the consecrated wafer is kept on an
altar in the church—"the abode and safe repository of their god."

Although at times a modern reader is likely to find parts of the
recitation more hilarious than horrifying, those readers of Oldham's
time opposed to the Court party must have found them sobering at

least. Loyola opens up the bag of tricks Rome's priests use to separate the faithful from their purses. In a wildly operatic kind of climax, he comes to the trumperies of the Mass and the Catholic doctrine of transubstantiation:

> Hey jingo, Sirs! What's this? 'tis bread you see?
> Presto, begone! 'tis now a deity.

As for confession:

> And here I might (if I durst) reveal
> What pranks are play'd in the confessional.

Then there is always the mock-epic catalog of the Inquisition, a hated Spanish institution:

> Should I tell all their countless knaveries,
> Their cheats and shams and forgeries and lies,
> Their cringings, crossings, censings, sprinklings, chrisms,
> Their conjurings and spells and exorcisms,
> Their motley habits, maniples, and stoles,
> Albs, amits, rochets, chimers, hoods, and cowls....

After his revelations of the infamies of the Roman religion and the faithlessness of the Jesuits, Loyola's image brings the satire to a frightening and abrupt conclusion with a mighty oath that calls down all sorts of disgusting things on himself, should he not be telling the truth. (His oath echoes that of Priapus in Horace's satire.) To avoid offending readers with delicate stomachs, only a few lines can be quoted. But these are enough to suggest the force of Oldham's abuse. The image protests the literal truth of his disclosures in lines like the following:

> If I have feigned in aught or broached a lie,
> Let worst of fates attend me—let me be
> Piss'd on by porter, groom, and oyster-whore,
> Or find my grave in jakes and common shore.

Even if we grant that in passages like these Oldham was working within the well-established convention of the "curse"—of which there are many examples in the volumes of *POAS*—we still must grant that he gives the lines a raw and distinctive vigor.

The Power of His Invective

A modern student must wonder if more sophisticated readers of Oldham's time were more amused by the nastiness, ingenuity, and inventiveness of this invective than they were moved by the warnings of the Catholic and Jesuit menace. Certainly, no matter how much the substance of the *Satires Upon the Jesuits* may seem little more than hysterical raving to a modern reader, he or she cannot help admiring the vigor and panache of the abuse. James Sutherland's assessment of the *Satires Upon the Jesuits* in the *Oxford History of English Literature* is a just one, although limited in its view. He writes:

The four satires are an exercise in sustained, and therefore monotonous invective. The abuse is continuous and unqualified, the voice is loud, emphatic, and brazenly confident; when we come to the last line of each satire we are conscious of a sudden cessation of noise.[29]

Ultimately, of course, we must raise questions about the *Satires Upon the Jesuits* that are of critical rather than of historical import, questions such as the following: Do the four satires taken together form a larger whole? Is there any progression from one satire to the next? Could the satires have been arranged in a different order without any impairment of total effect?

The fact is that a critic would have to exercise a good deal of ingenuity to find a coherent overall pattern or trace a discernible line of development in the satires as they stand. Oldham himself in an "Advertisement" (reprinted in Yale *POAS* II) made no great claims for originality or design. The first satire he "drew by Sylla's ghost on the great Jonson," a reference to Jonson's *Catiline*. In the second, the fire-breathing sermon, he "followed the swing of his own genius." The "design and some passages" of the third are based on Buchanan's sixteenth-century Latin satire on the Franciscans. The model for the last is "obvious to all that are anything acquainted with Horace."

What is noteworthy is that in his advertisement Oldham anticipates the charge that some of his readers will "tax him of buffoonery and turning holy things into ridicule." Some contemporaries, sympathetic with the goal of retaining some Catholicizing tendencies and influences within the Established Church, may very well have found some of his denunciations blasphemous and indefensible. But he reminds his readers that he is in the very position of the early Christian writers and apologists who railed at "the fopperies and superstitions of the heathens." His use of the term "heathens" is significant and contains an important clue. For Oldham, the Jesuits and their dangerous dupes had to be considered in the same light the early Christians considered heathens, creatures outside the law and the fold, the very embodiment of moral evil, fit only to be denounced and ridiculed. Thus, in the *Satires Upon the Jesuits* the heathenish ways of the Jesuits start with the ranting antics of Garnett who loves mischief and destruction for their own sakes. They deepen progressively until the last satire when we see the talking image of Loyola, likened to a phallic image of Priapus, cynically reviling all that is sacred to most Christians.

It would be foolhardy, however, to argue that there is a conscious overall design in the *Satires Upon the Jesuits*. Each of the satires, suitable for publication as a separate broadside, is a variation on a single theme. Whatever development there is, as indicated above, is capped when, like Priapus, Loyola condemns himself climactically in his own words.

Oldham lived out his short life in a century when, as James Sutherland remarks elsewhere, "men took sides with . . . passionate conviction."[30] His attack on the Jesuits displays this passionate, at times frenzied, partisanship. But today's reader, unfortunately, may come away from these satires with a sense of disappointment. He has been led to expect more than excited denunciation. Further, Oldham's over-reliance on vituperation and his inability to create a satiric mask and establish distance from his subject can wear on the nerves. Sutherland sums up the issue well in his study of satire in general just cited:

Oldham was much read in his own day; but his effectiveness depended to a large extent on political and religious passions which had only to be touched, like an exposed nerve, to produce an immediate reaction. We have our own exposed nerves in the twentieth century; but the religious one appears to be deadened, and our political troubles are of a very different order from those of Restoration England.[31]

As for political motives in the *Satires*, it is probably accurate to say as Brooks does, that they "contain nothing to further party purposes."[32] An early draft of the first of the satires did contain some lines attacking the Catholic Duke of York. But, Brooks reminds us, the publisher of the poems, Hindmarsh, was a well-known Tory under the patronage of the Duke of York. It must be noted also that the satires were begun while Oldham was living under the protection of Nicholas Carew, a Whig, but were continued in the household of Sir Edward Thurland, a Tory. The fact that Oldham later in his life humorously shrugged off the plot in his "The Careless Good Fellow" (1680)—"A plague of this fooling and plotting of late"— indicates that he may have worn his Whiggishness lightly.

Despite the tiresomeness of the fierce invective and unrelieved mercilessness of the vituperation, the *Satires Upon the Jesuits* have a crude vigor that can still hold our attention, especially when Oldham clusters a string of increasingly abusive nouns like a series of hammer blows. Lines like the following from the fourth of the satires, in which Oldham belabors the confessional, a favorite target of Protestant apologists, hold real sting:

> How you [Loyola's fellow Jesuits] at best advantages may buy
> Patents for sacrilege and simony;
> What tax is in the lech'ry office laid
> On panders, bawds, and whores that ply the trade. . . .

In addition, he manages to produce a genuine sense of outrage at the spectacle of the dying and unregenerate chief Jesuit addressing his followers in the third of the satires. Like Milton's Lucifer, the Jesuit leader shows an overweening pride in his own duplicity. We can appreciate the effect all this must have had on contemporary readers prepared to believe the worst of Catholics and Jesuits. As indicated earlier, the figure of Loyola arouses all the fears and commonly held suspicions of papistry by presenting them in the guise of "inside" information. What is really worthy of note, however, is that the *Satires Upon the Jesuits* do more than rekindle the stock fears and bugaboos concerning Catholicism—of which some still persist in our own time. As suggested earlier, Oldham cleverly appeals to the sturdy, rugged virtues of the uncomplicated Englishman by casting the Jesuit as a sly Machiavel, an amoral manipulator of "policy." With fear of an imminent return to Rome, and the memory of 1588 and the

Armada still alive, the satire shrewdly associates the Jesuits with the sly Italian and the ruthless Spaniard.

Sources of the *Satires Upon the Jesuits*

As we shall show later in this study, Oldham owed much of his success as a poet and satirist to his skills as an imitator. Scholarly attention has been paid to his sources, particularly the sources and the inspiration of his *Satires Upon the Jesuits*. The customary view, as expressed by the writers of the standard histories of literature—for example, C. W. Previté-Orton in the *Cambridge History of English Literature* (VII)—is that in much of his work Oldham is greatly indebted to Juvenal in a general way. Certainly there is no gainsaying the contemporary note this Roman writer's satire struck for Restoration readers and writers. The first of his satires, in particular, was widely admired and imitated. For example, Elias F. Mengel, Jr., editor of Yale *POAS* II, reports having collated as many as thirteen manuscript copies and two printed texts of a 1680 imitation of Juvenal's first satire attributed to Rochester in the original editions of *POAS* and in other collections. Lines like the following from this imitation (which is reprinted in the Yale *POAS* II) must have given the Roman poet's satire a familiar ring in a period of venal politicians and a corrupt Court:

> Who can abstain from satire in this age?
> What nature wants I find suppli'd by rage.
> Some do for pimping, some for treach'ry rise,
> But none's made great by being good or wise.
> Deserve a dungeon if you would be great,
> Rogues always are our ministers of state.
> Mean prostrate bitches, for a Bridewell fit,
> With England's wretched Queen must equal sit.

The reasons that Juvenal found for the satiric impulse in Silver Age Rome were the same ones that lent themselves to updating and adaptation in Oldham's times.

Another view is that Oldham was directly influenced by Boileau's *Le Lutrin*, which he was translating when he started the *Satires Upon the Jesuits*. (As we shall see, Oldham did other imitations of the French writer.) In *Le Lutrin* Boileau employed epic conventions, as Pope did later in *The Rape of the Lock*, to burlesque a silly, trivial incident, in this instance, a quarrel that had broken out among the canons of the Sainte Chapelle in Paris.

W. M. Williams has investigated the genesis of the *Satires Upon the Jesuits* in detail. On the basis of his study of Oldham's Bodleian notebook and workbooks, he argues that the poet was adapting to his own uses forms of political satire then current. The notebooks show, Williams reports, that Oldham had experimented with popular satiric modes, among them the formal curse, the formal exorcism, the "Advice to a Painter" (in which, as we noted earlier, an imaginary painter is advised how to portray an event or person), and the "vision," in which the ghost of a dead person, like that of Garnett in the first of the satires, appears. (All these forms are amply represented in the volumes of *POAS*.) Finally, Williams concludes, he hit upon the formal invective of the *Satires*, a form that unfortunately strikes later generations of readers as ineffective and strained, especially when measured against Dryden's achievement in *Absalom and Achitophel*.[33]

In another article Williams argues that Oldham was influenced by the satiric mode of Jonson's *Catiline* in satires other than the first of the *Satires Upon the Jesuits*. Hyperbole, shocking admissions of guilt—these are all devices found in *Catiline*, particularly in the first two acts. Thus, the argument goes, Oldham's vehemence derives not so much from the satires of Juvenal as it does ultimately from the tragedies of Seneca.[34] Oldham, as already noted, admired Jonson and composed an ode on his works. But when it comes to assessing the influence of Jonson on his work, we must keep in mind that he and the Elizabethan dramatist were both classicists and thus drew upon common sources, including Juvenal and other Roman writers. We must also remember that Oldham's admitted model for the third satire was Buchanan's *Franciscanus*, which also contains hyperbole and shocking admissions of guilt.

The Achievement of the *Satires Upon the Jesuits*

The *Satires Upon the Jesuits* do not represent political satire of a high order. They certainly fall far short of the controlled mastery of Dryden's *Absalom and Achitophel*. Only occasionally does the *saeva indignatio* of the great satirists shine through—in the third of the satires for the most part. Yet Oldham managed to create a framework against which his contemporaries could measure the full heinousness of the Popish Plot concocted by Oates and others and orchestrated so skillfully by the Earl of Shaftesbury.

Even in the eyes of some contemporaries, however, in an age when taste set no limits to vituperation, Oldham seemed to suffer from what Tom Brown, a poetaster and literary factotum of the time, called "his ungovernable heat." In his *Short Essay on English Satire* Brown notes that Oldham's

conceptions were noble, infinitely bold, full of fire and vivacity; he seldom was flat, and generally spoke to the purpose; he always was an enemy to vice, and encouraged the good and virtuous. Yet, on the other hand, it must be confess'd, that the same author was always in a passion; that he was inclinable to rail at every thing; that both his thoughts were too furious, and his style too bold to be correct, or to partake of those beauties which even his great master Juvenal did not think unworthy his care... 'Tis true, he expos'd and rail'd at vice; but then his pursuing both the theme and the persons too far, obliged the criminal he expos'd to believe that the sharpness of his Satire proceeded rather from some personal disgust, than any aversion to vice and immorality in general.

Oldham possessed a flair for casting himself in the role of stern prophet of the Old Testament. In the *Satires Upon the Jesuits* he took it upon himself to inveigh against evils no self-respecting Englishman would admit compromise with or tolerate in any measure. He made himself a national spokesman for the intense, albeit unreasoning, hatred of papistry and Jesuitry that almost silenced the voice of reason in the decade between 1678 and 1689.

His wild denunciations and bitter invective satisfied the public fancy for a time. His method, especially when compared with that of *Absalom and Achitophel,* is an artistically inferior one, and does not represent a satisfactory solution to what a modern scholar, Ruth Nevo, has identified as a major problem of seventeenth-century satire: that is, finding the proper place from which to attack, while at the same time retaining the appearance of the "heroic."[35] It is only fleetingly, if at all, that the figures of Garnett and Loyola take on the mold of Dryden's Achitophel (the earl of Shaftesbury) who remains uniformly heroic in his wrongdoing. Nonetheless, Mark Van Doren in his classic study, *John Dryden,* credits Oldham with being the first English satirist to treat specific contemporary affairs with dramatic grandeur and swelling dignity. He even goes so far as to say that Dryden's "stateliness" in *Absalom and Achitophel* derives, in part, from Loyola's speech in Oldham's third satire.[36]

Dryden's deft handling of the biblical analogue and his greater gifts as a poet impart to his villains a convincingly heroic stature, even though their essential villainy remains unsoftened. Oldham, however, is given to frenetic, if heroic, rant. He lacked, too, the technical resources of Dryden as a poet. For example, in some long passages of vituperation in the *Satires Upon the Jesuits*, his clumsy rhymes—even after we have allowed for differences in pronunciation in his time—give his couplets a roughness that detracts from the sought-after heroic quality. To anyone whose reading in the period has been confined to Dryden, lines such as the following from the first of the *Satires Upon the Jesuits* seem crude indeed:

> Never had Rome a nobler service done,
> Never had Hell; each day came thronging down
> Vast shoals of ghosts, and mine was pleas'd and glad,
> And smil'd when it the brave revenge survey'd.

Roger Sharrock, another modern writer on satire, makes a valid and perceptive point when he notes that in the *Satires Upon the Jesuits* Oldham says less about the facts of the Popish Plot than he does about "the state of mind in Protestant Englishmen." Quite unlike Dryden in *Absalom,* he shows "no grip" on the merits of the conflicting testimony in the Plot, or on the characters of the principals. In short, the basis of his attack is "generalized and not wholly imaginative." In charity to Oldham, Sharrock concludes that he shared the "popular superstitions about Popery," a sharing as he points out, that indicates a not surprising state of mind for a Protestant minister's son.[37]

Sharrock's comments should not be taken to mean that Oldham avoided, or was unable to employ, the specific and always fell back on the general. As we shall see, in his imitations of other writers, he could, indeed, make striking use of the specific detail from contemporary experience to illustrate a general principle or issue. Indeed, as Rachel Trickett states, he had a fondness for the specific:

Specific example is a familiar device for rousing rage in satire, and Oldham liked to use contemporary instances to sharpen indignation.[38]

In *Satires Upon the Jesuits* he had at hand a general issue, the Protestant Englishman's long-standing fear of Rome, capable of arousing rage in the breasts of many of his readers.

There is a refreshing element in Oldham's invective and generalized rage. A modern student is soon aware that he is dealing with not just another run-of-the-mill pallid imitation of Juvenal of which contemporary readers seemed never to tire. He had his faults, the chief of which is singled out in the judgment of James Sutherland, who remarks that the *Satires*

blaze like a bonfire in a dark and windy night. ... *Saeva indignatio* is very well in its way, but the more *saeva* the *indignatio*, the more a satirist must bring to his work a fine control, and men like Oldham give one the impression of being carried along on a horse that has bolted. ... [39]

Despite his lack of control, Oldham certainly has a place in literary history as an original imitator of Juvenal, Horace, and other satiric spirits. In fact he is one of those responsible for the development of a genre that reached its fullest and most polished state in the century after his, with the imitations of Pope and Johnson.

Chapter Four

The Arts of "Imitation"

The Example of the Ancients

Twentieth-century readers can find rather wearying the never-ending imitations of Horace, Juvenal, Martial, and Persius that poured from the pens of seventeenth- and eighteenth-century poets and poetasters. All any student need do, to discover how unfailing a fountain of inspiration for English imitators the Roman satirists were, is leaf cursorily through the appropriate volumes of Alexander Chalmers's *Works of the English Poets* (1810). The student, too, must constantly remind himself that most seventeenth- and eighteenth-century readers of Oldham, Dryden, and Pope shared at least a nodding acquaintance with the classical writers, especially the Romans. Classical models were often the one measure against which current productions were gauged. One problem for a modern reader is that full appreciation of the imitation presupposes some familiarity with the originals. David Vieth, perhaps, overstates this point only slightly when in discussing Rochester's *An Allusion to Horace, the Tenth Satyr of the First Book* (1675–76), "the first such work in the English language," he says:

Based on Horace, *Satires* I. 10, it requires a knowledge of the Latin original so that the reader will be aware, not only of clever adaptations of Roman circumstances to English ones, but of ironic discrepancies between the two.[1]

There is no doubt that a serious-minded student must have at hand the appropriate volumes from the Loeb Classical Library when reading Oldham or other imitators of classical models.

As students of seventeenth- and eighteenth-century literature are well aware, interest in the classics, especially the Roman ones, did not confine itself to a search for rhetorical models to be imitated. Ancient Rome and the London of Oldham's time were thought to share in common certain character types, as well as certain habits and practices of the Court and the merchant classes. In time, inventive spirits in France and England developed a form of adaptation known properly as the "imitation." As Harold Love remarks in an essay entitled "Rochester and the Traditions of Satire," it was Horace's disciple Boileau who was "the first major seventeenth-century satirist to attempt a rigorous re-creation of classical models."[2] Samuel Johnson, in an oft-quoted comment in the life of Rochester in his *Lives of the Poets*, notes that during the reign of Charles II there "began that adaptation, which has since been frequent, of ancient poetry to present times."

This re-creation, or imitation, was to become a popular form in the next century and, indeed, became a favorite form of Johnson himself, whose *London* is a prime example of it. During the Restoration, Oldham was among the first to naturalize characters and circumstances drawn from Latin originals in his imitations. Even though the *Satires Upon the Jesuits* are primarily an exercise in invective and, in a formal sense, little more than an extended lampoon, much of the pleasure cultivated readers derived from reading them came from recognizing sources imitated, especially in the first and fourth satires.

In his "Advertisement" to the *Satires Upon the Jesuits* Oldham was careful to establish a classical pedigree for the work. Interestingly enough, and in accord with his leanings toward the direct and the scurrilous, he forestalls any criticism of his handling of sources and his own scholarship by dismissing discussion of the "original, progress, and rules of satire," a staple of heavy-handed introductions of the time, as frivolous pedantry. Although he assures his readers that he is acquainted with the theories of a Renaissance critic like Isaac Casaubon, as well as of other humanists, his chief concern, he implies, is the serious social and political evil that occasioned his satire.

Nonetheless, the *Satires Upon the Jesuits* were designed in part, to be imitations of Persius, Juvenal, and Horace. He hoped to keep himself and his inflammatory material under better control by placing them, as did other poets of the time, within the framework of recognizable and much-revered sources—and relating the sources to contemporary situations or personages.

Someone who knows Oldham only from the brief accounts of him in the histories of literature may think of him only as a master of the abusive, with a pronounced talent for loud vituperation, no matter what its provenance. But he was more than a scolding blusterer. Instead, when his work is read and considered as a whole, he appears, rather, as a critic of men and their ways who managed with skill to adapt classical and later models to his own topical purposes, while at the same time retaining his own strong, coarse, and original satiric bent. As we noted earlier, his *Satire Against Virtue*, which shocked some contemporaries with its indelicacy—and helped win him the favor and attention of the Restoration Court Wits—shows this combination of qualities. Whenever he worked without reference to a suitable model, as in his *Satire Upon a Woman*, he could become genuinely nasty. Into this work he weaves rather disgusting variations on the theme of woman's innate depravity—a generalized theme passed on from classical sources to patristic writers, and down the centuries to countless divines and their countless sermons.

The two poems just named, in which he plays variations on popular and general themes and adopts the conventions of dramatic writing, are, however, in the manner most historians of literature ascribe to Oldham, a manner distinguished by rant and disfigured by ugly detail. Some lines of the *Satire Against Virtue*, a work already discussed at some length, seem almost an unwitting burlesque of the rant of villains of the heroic plays of the seventeenth century. The overall strategy, as we have seen, is the employment of a "turnabout," with the speaker in the satire extolling viciousness— with recognizable irony, the author hopes. In the hands of Swift or Fielding, this technique can be a devastating one. Unfortunately, many of Oldham's readers missed his irony—understandably, since it is clumsily handled. We have already noted how Anthony Wood charged the author of *A Satire Against Virtue* with being a "Mad, Ranting, Blasphemous, and Debauched Writer." Oldham's irony is simply too heavy-handed.

The Satire Upon a Woman, along with the *Satire Against Virtue*, one of the works Bell felt to be too indecorous to be included in his edition, stands with the *Satire Upon a Printer* and *Upon a Lady, Who By Overturning of a Coach Had her Coats Behind Flung Up*, as a typical example of the poet's more unpleasant vein. In his attack of womankind he reasserts, as has already been indicated, an age-old libel, namely, that the woman tends naturally toward depravity. Oldham undoubtedly was acquainted with memorable expressions given the theme by Juvenal and Martial, particularly by the former in his notorious Sixth Satire. The woman, Oldham argues, possesses "within a gaudy case, a nasty soul." His attack is little more than a long convoluted curse filled out with revolting physical details.

Can we determine that Oldham really shared the view that woman by nature is unregenerate? Certainly in his time, as in any other, examples of female unregeneracy were to be found. But in an age when educated readers shared a common education in the classics, or professed a common reverence for them, one concludes that in this instance Oldham was doing little more than mining the classical heritage for stock ideas and attitudes that he could apply to the social scene of his own age. Oldham was one of the more accomplished of the satiric writers of his time who never tired of imitating or alluding to Juvenal and Horace, finding the undesirable types decried by Roman satirists—the social climber, the parasite, the scheming woman—reembodied in Restoration society.

Oldham as Imitator: An Overview

It is unfortunate that most students of the period seldom get beyond the more loudly abusive works of Oldham like the *Satires Upon the Jesuits*, for it is in his imitations of Horace and Juvenal and a writer of his own century, Boileau, that he can be most readable. He also tried his hand at imitating other than satiric models, paraphrasing and adapting works of Virgil, Ovid, and the Greek poets Anacreon, Bion, and Moschus, as well as biblical texts.

Taken as a whole, his attempts at the imitation are uneven in quality. But as Sutherland states,

. . . it is in . . . adaptations of an ancient poet to the modern world that his chief claim to historical importance lies.[3]

John Butt, in the introduction to Volume 4 of the Twickenham edition of the poems of Alexander Pope, comments that Oldham "shows consciousness of doing what had not been done before."[4] Consciously or not, he certainly was one of the first to set out to write imitations of the kind we associate with Dryden and Pope. When it comes to assigning credit for having been the first, we must bear in mind that, as an earlier citation indicates, David Vieth contends that Rochester's *Allusion to Horace, the Tenth Satire,* composed about 1675, is the first imitation in the sense that Pope's adaptations of Horace in the next century are "imitations."

Both faithful translations and paraphrases of favorite classical texts were much in vogue in Oldham's time, as we have noted. For example, he was only one of many poets and academics who tried their hands at rendering into English Horace's much-glossed and highly respected *Art of Poetry*. His *Horace's Art of Poetry Imitated in English*, though for the most part lacking in urbanity and felicity of expression, does demonstrate his methods and shows how his practice foreshadows the more elegant practice of Pope. In a preface Oldham acknowledges his presumptuousness in offering a new version of the *Art of Poetry* after earlier ones by Ben Jonson and the Earl of Roscommon. But he announces that the imitation was a chore forced upon him, a claim that, Brooks points out, stemmed from a poem written by Sir William Soames taking him to task for his authorship of the pornographic *Sardanapalus*. Soames's attack, contained in a British Museum manuscript copy of the obscene poem and also printed anonymously in London in *Examen Poeticum* (1693), contains the following ill-natured lines addressed to a schoolmaster as much in need of instruction as his pupils:

> From the Boys hands, take Horace into Thine,
> And thy rude Satyrs, by his Rules, refine.[5]

Our concern, however, is not with what occasioned the English version, but with the fact that Oldham indicates in the preface that he knew what he was about—"imitating" rather than simply translating Horace. He asserts that his objective is to make the Roman poet speak as if he were alive, and

Alter the scene from Rome to London and . . . make use of English names . . . when the parallel would decently permit. . . .

This adapting a text to later times and conditions is what distinguishes the method of the imitator from that of the translator. Indeed, in the *Life of Pope* Samuel Johnson, with the rendering of the *Art of Poetry* in mind, credits Oldham with having been an originator of the imitation as a literary form. The statement deserves quotation in full:

This mode of imitation, in which the ancients are familiarised, by adapting their sentiments to modern topics, by making Horace say of Shakespeare what he originally said of Ennius, and accommodating his satires on Pantoldus and Nometanus to the flatterers and prodigals of his own time, was first practised in the reign of Charles the Second by Oldham and Rochester, at least I remember no instances more ancient. It is a kind of middle composition between translation and original design, which pleases when the thoughts are unexpectedly applicable, and the parallels lucky.[6]

Oldham, as Brooks remarks, underwent something like a "Horatian phase in his work" starting with the last of the *Satires Upon the Jesuits*, in which he took Horace's Eighth Satire as a model.[7] This was a phase wherein he attempted to "familiarise" Horace, as Johnson put it.

Unfortunately for Oldham, his imitations in the Horatian vein too often suffer when compared with those of Rochester or Dryden. Rochester's "Allusion to Horace, the Tenth Satyr of the First Book," the work that David Vieth regards as the first of the imitations, has a lightness of touch that Oldham seldom achieved. It naturalizes references to English poets, taking Dryden to task as Horace takes Lucilius to task in the original, while retaining the basic structure of the Latin original. As for Dryden, his satiric purpose, compared with Oldham's, was broader in scope and more humane in its concerns, that is, more Horatian than Juvenalian. "The true end of satire is the amendment of vices by correction," Dryden announced in the dedication to the translation of the *Aeneid.* On the other hand, as the *Satires Upon the Jesuits* amply demonstrate, Oldham's impulse was to flay an enemy mercilessly. He saw enemies, like the Jesuits, as beyond hope of redemption, any chance of correction. Although, in accord with the taste of the time, Dryden's attack could be fierce at times, its sting usually came from indirection, underplayed irony, graceful turns of phrase, and, as in *Absalom and Achitophel*, from clever use of analogue. We need compare only Dryden's ironic description of Corah (Titus Oates) with a sample of Oldham's abuse of a favorite foe in the second of the *Satires Upon the Jesuits*. Here is Dryden's Oates, an almost comic figure:

> Sunk were his eyes, his voice was harsh and loud,
> Sure signs he neither choleric was nor proud.
> His long chin prov'd his wit; his saintlike grace
> A church vermilion, and a Moses' face.
>
> (ll. 646–49)

As for Oldham's Jesuit, he is evil beyond all recall, as these lines

from the second of the *Satires Upon the Jesuits*, quoted earlier, make
clear:

> Believe bawds modest, and shameless stews;
> And binding drunkards' oaths, and strumpets' vows;
> And when in time these contradictions meet,
> Then hope to find 'em in a Loyolite.

Without doubt, as an imitator of ancient writers, Oldham was
at home with a model like Juvenal. Overall, his natural bent, as has
already been demonstrated, was for the direct attack. Nonetheless,
his imitations in a softer vein are worthy of attention.

A Softer Vein

His range of imitations and paraphrases in a non-Juvenalian mode
is fairly broad, with results ranging from the praiseworthy to the
undistinguished. He wrote imitations of the Greek lyric poets Anacreon, Bion, and Moschus; he tried his hand at passages from Ovid's
Metamorphoses, as well as passages from Virgil, Catullus, and Petronius; he even wrote several adaptations of the Psalms.

"Bion, a Pastoral," "written in imitation of Moschus and occasioned by the death of Rochester," leaves a reader with a deeper
appreciation of the genius of Milton, whose *Lycidas* is so magnificent
an English adaptation of the artificial conventions of the pastoral
elegy. As his contemporaries agreed, Oldham lacked the softer lyric
touch and the Virgilian elegance required for success with the form,
an exotic one in English. Every student recalls Dr. Johnson's dislike
of the pastoral in general and of *Lycidas* in particular, and his memorable comment in the life of Milton that "Passion plucks no berries
from the myrtle or ivy."

This unsympathetic comment applies to Oldham's "Bion," as
well as to his "Lamentation for Adonis," an imitation of "Bion."
The former (complete title: "Bion, a Pastoral Imitation of the
Greek of Moschus, bewailing the death of the Earl of Rochester")
does have a few good moments. Despite the highly artificial devices
of the pastoral elegy, contemporary readers, well aware of Rochester's
great gifts, were probably moved by the consoling thought that his
voice could "charm Proserpine" and return him to the land of the
living, as Eurydice was returned from the shades. Oldham's version
of the melancholy refrain is not without charm:

> Come, all ye muses, come, adorn the shepherd's hearse,
> With never fading garland, never dying verse.

On the whole, however, neither "Bion" nor the "Lamentation for Adonis" rises much above the level of the school exercise.

Likewise, Oldham, as an imitator and translator, was not quite up to meeting the demands of Ovid's "Passion of Byblis." This tale, found in Book 9 of the *Metamorphoses*, recounts the guilty love of Byblis for her brother Caunus. The story is typically Ovidian, with its warning, made especially disingenuous in Oldham's version, to "heedless maids" to "shun forbidden love," followed by an unraveling in luscious detail of the sister's illicit desire for her twin brother. (Needless to say, Bell omits this imitation from his edition.)

The brother and sister of the tale were the children of Miletus, who had been driven from Crete by Minos. Byblis's passion, as Ovid relates, is nourished in secret, and grows and grows until, quite overcome by it, she sends a servant to her brother Caunus with a letter confessing her love and entreating him to seduce her. Even though he expresses genuine horror at the proposal, she still confronts him, clings to him, and pleads with him to make her his mistress. She remains so insistent that Caunus has no choice but to flee. Driven to madness by her unnatural and unrequited love, Byblis herself wanders until, after weeping unceasingly, she is turned into a fountain by the nymphs.

Ovid tells this unpleasant story in rich language. Oldham, who carries the tale only up to the point where Byblis has received word that her brother spurns her offer and, more than that, is horrified by it, simply lacked the resources to suggest the melody and lushness of Ovid's language. When, for example, he describes the girl's guilty dreams of being ravished by her brother, his expression is flat, filled out with stock epithets:

> .   .   .   Gods,
> What a scene of joy was that:
> How fast I clasp'd the vision to my panting breast.

The imitation, however, struck favorably the ears of some readers closer to his own time. The critic John Dennis, the implacable foe of Pope, saw fit, in his "Preface to the Passion of Byblis," to apologize for his own translation of the tale after Oldham's. Some readers,

he feared, "will never forgive me the attempting it after him."
Nonetheless, Dennis—and a twentieth-century reader concurs—re-
marked that Oldham lacked the delicacy, "the tenderness of soul,"
for the task.

Oldham probably undertook some of these softer nonsatiric themes
simply because such tasks were *de rigueur* in witty circles. Since the
Court Wits were themselves dedicated to the pursuit of wine and
women, they enjoyed in particular gracefully wrought imitations of
the more shocking and lubricious works of the Greek and Roman
poets. The Earl of Rochester adapted Ovid and Petronius and wrote
a drinking song in the manner of Anacreon. Oldham likewise turned
into English an ode of Anacreon in which is expressed a desire for
a cup that will be to the confirmed drinker what carved and em-
blazoned armor is to the mighty warrior. In his rendering, Oldham
asks for

> .   .   .   a mighty bowl
> Large as my capacious soul.

The cup is to be decorated not with martial scenes, but with figures
of Bacchus and Cupid, deities more suggestive of the territories to
be conquered through the "mighty bowl."

Oldham's imitations, it must be conceded, fall far short of Rochester's in expressing moral abandon and satiety. Only infrequently, as
in the imitation of a passage from Petronius ("Fragment of Petronius
Paraphras'd") does he give memorable expression to the melancholy that, as rakes and moralists alike tell us, always succeeds over-
indulgence in pleasures of the senses. The fragment in question
plays a variation on the theme of a lover left *post coitum tristis.*
He tries to prolong anticipation and delay "fruition,"

> That with a moment takes its flight.

Among other works of Ovid that Oldham imitated are elegies—
the fourth, fifth, and tenth of the Second Book of the *Amores*
("Some Elegies Out of Ovid's Amours Imitated")—that must have
appealed to courtly rakes of the time. In the fourth elegy the Roman
poet confesses to an unconquerable weakness for women and the
pleasures of Venus. The fifth elegy revolves about a lover's jealousy

and describes his distress as he imagines his mistress giving herself to another. The tenth deals with the age-old, and still unresolved, problem of the lover who is in love with more than one woman at the same time. Oldham, unfortunately, was ill suited for imitations of this kind. The following lines, in their pedestrian quality, typify his efforts:

> Wheree'er I cast my looks abroad
> In every place I find temptation strow'd.

He lacked Rochester's elegance of phrase, rhythmic smoothness, and world-weary amorality of tone. In addition, Ovid, unlike Horace or Juvenal, seldom affords him opportunity for topicality and the adaptation of character and incident to the contemporary London scene, the very elements that became his strong points in satire. Virgil likewise remained quite beyond his reach. He tried his hand at the *Eighth Ecologue*, in which the shepherd Damon bewails the infidelity of his beloved Nisa who will wed Mopsus. In his attempt to suggest the cadence of the original refrain, which in the Latin has a lovely, haunting quality, he imprudently carries the dactyls over into English with little success, producing only an inappropriately jingling meter:

> Strike up my pipe, play me in tempered strain
> What I have sung on the Maenalian plain.

He is at his worst as an imitator or close translator in lyric forms, as is shown in his rendering of Catullus's *Epigram* III, the famous and often-imitated address to Lesbia (*"vivamus, mea Lesbia, atque amemus"*) in which, with the thought of the endless night of death approaching, the poet pleads for an endless round of kisses—*"Da mi basia mille"*—in Oldham's version heavy-footed and ill-rhymed:

> Nay, Lesbia, never ask me this
> How many kisses will suffice.

His tendency, as the just-quoted lines indicate, was to smother the original lyric concision with clumsy expansions and circumlocutions.

Attempts at the Pindaric

Not surprisingly, Oldham fared only indifferently, as well, with the Pindaric, a loose form which was popular at the time and a challenge to versifiers, especially after the publication of Abraham Cowley's *Pindarique Odes* in 1656. As we noted earlier, he tried his hand at this unnatural form in English early in his career in his reasonably successful elegy on the death of his friend Morwent. On the whole, Horace's well-known warning to all who presume to emulate Pindar can be applied to Oldham, as well as to other seventeenth-century composers of Pindarics. As the Roman poet counsels (*Ode*, IV 2), whoever is rash enough to follow Pindar soars in the sun with the waxen wings of Daedalus and, like Icarus, is doomed to plunge into the heartless sea. Pindar himself, Horace remarks, escaped this fate because his verse sweeps along unimpeded like a rain-swollen mountain stream over its banks. One of a kind, he must be awarded Apollo's laurels, even when he throws off the restraint of the rules.

Although for Pindar the ode was a regular, if highly elaborate, form associated with the dance, for Cowley and other English imitators it became a relatively free form, allowing, as Brooks describes it, for

unexhausted abundance of invention; noble extravagance; an "enthusiastical" manner, falling boldly from one thing into another with disregard of transition and a readiness to digress; all are matched with an equal bravura in hyperbole, simile, and extended metaphor that partakes of simile.[8]

The freedom, or, as some thought, license, with which Pindar was imitated led William Congreve to complain later, in his *Discourse on the Pindaric Ode* (1706), that Cowley, though not to be held responsible,

...may have been the principal, though innocent, occasion of so many deformed poems. ...

Oldham was far from equal to the task of employing the Pindaric successfully, even though for the most part, whatever of his verse is not in heroic couplets is in Pindarics. To see him at his best in this artificial form, we must look again at the earliest of his poems that can be traced to a definite date, the already discussed *To the Memory of My dear Friend Mr. Charles Morwent,* written in 1675, when he was only twenty. The elegy is long and labored, containing forty-two stanzas of varying length. Robert Bell professed to find much merit in it, influenced, perhaps, by Alexander Pope's having marked it as one of the poems worthy of commendation in the copy of Oldham's works he owned. Bell's comment singles out the elements that must have made Oldham appear as a young man of promise in the eyes of contemporaries. The work

is carefully constructed on the models then in vogue, and shows considerable skill in the exhaustive process of extravagant panegyric. The germs of future excellence strike root boldly in this piece, which is remarkable for variety and fertility of illustration, and has many passages of sweetness and beauty.[9]

The poem is indeed a worthy representative of the Pindaric "models then in vogue," although it strikes modern ears as a strained and somewhat tedious venture in the panegyric and elegiac traditions. Nonetheless, it must be admitted, despite the artificiality of the conventions involved—e.g., the affectation of a grief too deep to be expressed, the fictive mourning of all nature at the loss ("The day in funeral blackness mourned"), the catalog of the departed one's truly heroic virtues, the ritual change of mood from grief to jubilation occasioned by the climactic apotheosis of the deceased one ("Go, happy soul, ascend the joyful sky")—there is considerable genuine feeling. In addition, in spite of its repetitiousness, this elaborate poem does, indeed, display signs of poetic ingenuity, especially in the development of an occasional figure. Stanza 32, for example, contains a worthy example of metaphysical wit—the inevitable compass— and is deserving of quotation, if only to suggest the flavor of the lament and the complications of the Pindaric form:

> Hence, though at once thy soul lived here and there,
> Yet heaven alone in its thoughts did share;
> It owned no home, but in the active sphere.
> Its notions always did to that bright center roll,
> And seemed to inform thee only on parole.
> Look how the needle does to its dear north incline,
> As, wer't not fixed, 'twould to that region climb;
>   Or mark what hidden force

Bids the flame upwards take its course,
And makes it with that swiftness rise
As if 'twere winged by the air through which it flies.
Such a strong virtue did thy inclinations bend,
And made them still to the blest mansions tend.
That mighty slave, whom the proud victor's rage
Shut prisoner in a golden cage,
Condemned to glorious vassalage,
Ne'er longed for dear enlargement more,
Nor his gay bondage with less patience bore,
Than this great spirit brooked its tedious stay,
While fettered here in brittle clay,
And wished to disengage and fly away.
It vexed and chafed, and still desired to be
Released to the sweet freedom of eternity.

The *Praise of Homer*, suggested by Cowley's *The Praise of Pindar*, and another work mentioned earlier, *Upon the Works of Ben Jonson*, can also be regarded as odes representative of Oldham's efforts in the free-flowing Pindaric form. The first of these is a labored exercise for the most part, flawed by feeble and jarring approximate rhymes, even after a modern reader has made due allowances for changes in the sounds of English since the seventeenth century. The ode, revolving about the Renaissance idolatry of the ancients, opens with the customary apostrophe to its subject. It gives the same advice that Pope was later to incorporate into his *Essay on Criticism* in far more polished turns of phrase: an admonition to the reader to honor Homer

Whom we acknowledge our sole text, and holy writ;
None other judge infallible we own.

Though physically blind, the argument goes on, Homer was a real seer, teaching all ages how both to study and to follow nature. Inspirer of men of action and men of achievement, including the great Alexander himself, every nation would be proud to claim him for its own. His works will far outlast the works of most men.

The most interesting stanza in this generally mediocre work is the one in which Oldham bewails the insularity imposed on the English poet and deplores the lot of

> thy British offspring here,
> Who strive by thy great model monuments to rear.

An English descendant of Homer toils to enrich his countrymen, but is condemned not to be understood beyond the narrow confines of his island. He is even despised by some (the French critics?) for his language:

> In vain for worthless fame we toil,
> Who're pent in the straight limits of a narrow isle;
> In vain our force and art we spend
> With noble labour to enrich our land,
> Which none beyond our shores vouchsafe to understand.
> Be the fair structure ne'er so well designed,
> The parts with ne'er so much proportion joined,
> Yet foreign bards (such is their pride or prejudice)
> All the choice workmanship for the materials' sake despise.

This is a revealing confession of provincialism, one effect, undoubtedly, of Charles II's and his courtiers' long stay in France and the influence of French culture on the Court. Homer is far more fortunate than an English poet in that he is understood and admired, and his language is understood and admired, in every civilized nation:

> In language universal as thy sense.

The poem in praise of another poet, Ben Jonson (*Upon the Works of Ben Jonson*), is by far Oldham's best effort in the Pindaric vein. One reason for this is that he felt a special affinity for the Elizabethan poet, who also had a talent for heaping abuse and scorn on the follies of his fellowmen and whose mission as a satirist and comic writer was to castigate the manners and morals of mankind by holding them up to ridicule. (As noted earlier, a scene in Jonson's tragedy *Catiline* provided a model for a section of one of the *Satires Upon the Jesuits*.) In the opening apostrophe Oldham expresses his bitterness at the neglect of Jonson only a quarter of a century or so after his death:

> Great Thou! whom 'tis a crime almost to dare to praise.

For him, Jonson is nothing less than "the founder of our stage,"
since it was he who brought order and regularity to the "rude and
undigested lump" that was the English stage before his arrival on
the theatrical scene. Like other poets—Oldham has Shakespeare in
mind—Jonson was possessed of a divine frenzy and rage, but it was
a "managed rage" that put itself under the governance of reason so
much so that

> Nature and art, together met and joined,
> Made up the character of thy great mind.

Further, Jonson was no mere adapter of foreign models. Rather,
his was a muse of sturdy native growth:

> But staple all, and all of English growth and make.

He was well "skilled and read in human kind," well acquainted with
the humors of men. His characters, in their "humors," disclose his
solid knowledge of human nature and its foibles. Whatever models
he followed, he made entirely his own. Fancied by his enemies to
be slow and plodding, he only appears less facile in his craft because
he was careful and deliberate. Responding, undoubtedly, to criticism
of this kind that he himself had received from his contemporaries,
Oldham asserts that this is a fault he is glad to share with his master:

> Let me (with pride so to be guilty thought)
> Share all thy wished reproach, and share thy shame,
> If diligence be deemed a fault.

All in all, the critical estimate of Jonson in the poem is a just
one, shared and confirmed by the judgment of later ages. A reader
is made aware that Oldham was proud to see himself as akin to
the stiff and unbending playwright who, too, was above courting
popular acclaim. In the following lines Oldham is speaking of himself, as well as of Jonson:

> Let meaner spirits stoop to low precarious fame,
> Content on gross and coarse applause to live,
> And what the dull and senseless rabble give;
> Thou didst it still with noble scorn condemn.

In his *Letter from the Country to a Friend in Town*, written in 1678 probably not long after the Pindaric on Jonson, Oldham gives expression again to his disdain of popular applause. In this verse epistle, cast in the manner of Horatian satire and composed in heroic couplets, he describes for a friend the disappointments and the frustrations that accompany the pursuit of the Muse. Fame and fortune are often purchased, he says, only at the cost of one's integrity. He announces defiantly:

> Let wealth and honour be for fortune's slaves,
> The alms of fools, and prize of crafty knaves.

As for him,

> Rich or a beggar, free or in the Fleet,
> What'er my fate is, 'tis my fate to write.

His muse, like that of Jonson or a Roman satirist, was an independent and rugged one that he served with full dedication, despite adversity and lack of acclaim.

The "Roman" Poet

Oldham's steadfastness of purpose and defiance of ill fortune imparted qualities to his work that have enabled it to survive, despite its all too frequent bombast and clumsiness. His bluntness of manner and his habitual scorn of the common taste helped make adapting and imitating Roman satirists completely to his liking. In addition, his attempt to adapt a poet like Horace to the tastes of his own time was, whether he intended it to be or not, one sure way to attract the attention of the influential wits. Cultivated readers were fond of verse criticisms of life, art, and manners in the Horatian manner. Readers never seemed to tire, for example, of translations and imitations of the *Ars Poetica*, which, as we have already noted, Oldham adapted to English. In 1680, a year before Oldham's version appeared, the Earl of Roscommon had presented his much-praised translation. Nor did these satisfy the readers' appetite. John Sheffield's *Essay Upon Poetry* followed in 1682, and itself was followed a year later by Boileau's famous Horatian verse epistle, *L'Art Poétique*.

Still other excellent versions were produced by Sir William Soames and John Dryden, among others.

From any standpoint, Oldham's imitation of Horace's famous epistle is a creditable performance. Brooks argues, for example, that some of Pope's lines are indebted to some of Oldham's in this adaptation.[10] The original four hundred and seventy-six lines, as found in the Loeb edition, are expanded to slightly more than eight hundred. His expansions succeed in giving the adaptation a contemporary ring, with its allusions to English writers and English manners. Thus, when rendering Horace's famous lines admonishing would-be writers to eschew putting inappropriate words into the mouths of their speakers, Oldham finds up-to-date and timely references:

> Let them not speak, like burlesque characters
> The wit of Billingsgate and Temple-stairs.

Or when Horace prescribes that no play be shorter or longer than five acts, if its authors hope for more than one performance, Oldham adds a reference to theatrical practice of his time:

> Five acts, no more nor less, your play must have,
> If you'll a handsome third day's share receive.

His readers were well aware that a run of at least three days was a matter of consuming interest to a playwright, since the third night's receipts went to the author.

Even as he translates rather literally, he manages to capture the distinctive vigor of the original, as when Achilles is brought on stage—

> Let him be fierce and brave, all heat and rage,
> Inflexible and headstrong to all laws....

While remaining idiomatic, these lines are so contrived as to approximate the delightfully fierce and heavy-footed movement of the polysyllabic epithets Horace applies to the raging Achilles:

> Impiger, iracundus, inexorabilis, acer....

The touchstone, of course, is the rendering of celebrated passages of the original so often quoted because of their succinctness and elegance. Thus, the well-known "parturient montes, nascetur ridiculus mus" becomes in Oldham's version the equally straightforward and crisp,

> You look for mountains, and out creeps a mouse.

Some of the more freely adapted passages manage to blend the spirit of the original with a fresh contemporary flavor. The following lines, deserving quotation at length, exemplify this. In them Oldham catches the tone of the original epistle in which Horace talks about rules of versification, while at the same time giving a rather unpromising topic an interesting treatment—at least for readers of the time who took rules for writing seriously:

> But will you therefore be so much a fool
> To write at random, and neglect a rule?
> Or, while your faults are set to general view,
> Hope all men should be blind, or pardon you?
> Who would not such foolhardiness condemn,
> Where, though perchance you may escape from blame,
> Yet praise you never can expect, or claim?
> Therefore be sure you study to apply
> To the great patterns of antiquity;
> Ne'er lay the Greeks and Romans out of sight,
> Ply them by day, and think on them by night.

Unfortunately, it is true that the last two lines lack the polish and melody of the original Latin ("vos exemplaria Graeca nocturna manu, versate diurna") or the grace of Pope's well-known rendering in the *Essay on Criticism* ("Be Homer's works your study and delight, / Read them by day, and meditate by night"). Nonetheless, Oldham is "imitating," rather than merely paraphrasing. His Horace has the voice of a Restoration poet.

As has been repeatedly stated or implied, the test of an imitator's art lies in his ability to give the source imitated an authentically "contemporary" ring. Oldham can rise to the occasion when he is adapting the social criticism of the Roman satirists to his own time. James Sutherland argues convincingly that he was most successful with Horace's *Ninth Satire of the First Book* ("Ibam forte via sacra. . . ."), even going so far as to call Oldham's rendering of this

a little masterpiece, beautifully lively and colloquial; a Restoration poem
that happened to be written by a Latin poet sixteen hundred years earlier.[11]

This is also one of the imitations that Pope singled out for praise
in his copy of Oldham's works. What is especially pleasing about
this version of Horace's complaints about a type of big-city pest is
that its content, in Samuel Johnson's expression, is "familiarised."
For that matter, the obnoxious creature in the satire who attached
himself to Horace as the poet strolled in ancient Rome is a type
peculiar to no one age. He was as familiar to readers of Oldham's
time as he is to readers of today.

Oldham's method with the *Ninth Satire* ("The Impertinent") is
to expand upon the original and find clever contemporary applications. While Horace's bore merely sidles up and annoys the poet with
small talk and gossip as he strolls, Oldham's becomes a Restoration
fop who introduces the topics that made up the daily small talk of
Londoners: Newgate, the need for rain, the current price of hay, a
comet recently sighted over the Hague. All the while, the reader
who remembers his Horace discerns in the imitation the underlying
pattern of the original satire—for example, the walk past the law
courts—and is aware that Horace's patron Maecenas has been trans-
formed into a Restoration "his Grace." These are the general features
that made imitations so pleasurable for and popular with readers
of the seventeenth and eighteenth centuries: a clever combining of
the old and the new, with recollected scenes from the classical past
forming the backdrop against which contemporary variations are
played. Above all, there was the unspoken and unquestioned assump-
tion that Augustan Rome and Restoration England had much in
common, including, of course, similar parasitic types.

As the speaker in Oldham's imitation walks along the Mall, the
foppish bore falls in with him and

> . . . all the while baits me with tedious chat,
> Speaks much about the drought, and how the rate
> Of hay is raised, and what it now goes at;
> Tells me of a new comet at the Hague,
> Portending God knows what, a dearth, or plague,
> Names every wench that passes through the park,
> How much she is allowed, and who the spark.

He runs through other topics currently exercising Londoners, including the Popish Plot and the frenzy surrounding it:

> Next he begins to plague me with the plot,
> Asks, whether I were known to Oates or not.

The speaker's rugged honesty is opposed, in terms contemporary readers could well appreciate, to the presumption and hypocrisy of the parasite who dogs his steps through the park, badgering him the while with questions in the misplaced hope of using him as means to curry favor with the rich and powerful. The hanger-on is a recognizable social type that infests big cities of all ages. Nowadays such a person is likely to be in public relations or press agentry, foisting himself at cocktail parties on people he considers important.

Oldham, however, is on the whole, much less successful in his imitations of Horace's odes than he is in the imitation of some of the satires. Unfortunately, he lacked a sensitivity for the meditative or reflective, as is shown by his awkward attempt to render Horace's exquisite plaint on the flight of time and the inevitability of death in *Ode* xiv of the Second Book ("Eheu fugaces, Postume, Postume, labuntur anni"). The mellow, lapidary quality of the original is in no way suggested by Oldham's heavy-handed Pindaric, as, among other things, the unfortunate use of "to bribe" in the opening lines makes clear:

> Alas! dear friend, alas! time hastes away,
> Nor is it in our power to bribe its stay;

Oldham also essayed an imitation of Horace's well-known *Ode* xxxi of the First Book—often called "The Poet's Prayer"—an elegantly turned set of alcaics in which the Roman poet asks Apollo not for wealth and luxury, but for contentment with a simple lot and the greater good of an old age with a sound mind and a sound body. Besides standing as a challenge to any poet of the time who knew his Horace, the subject of the ode must have seemed particularly inviting to Oldham, and the adaptation one he relished undertaking in view of the hardness of his life as a struggling young poet. His version, however, can hardly be deemed a triumph. He expands Horace's tightly compressed and understated twenty lines into an ode

of forty-six lines, divided into three sections, two of fourteen, and
one of eighteen lines. Again, his method is to "familiarise." Just as
Horace, for example, renounces all interest in Italian farms, rich
cargoes, and stores of wine, he declares he has no interest in the
items of wealth familiar to the readers of his age. When Horace
mentions briefly wines for which Syrian traders bartered, Oldham
runs through a list of the wines fancied by the wealthy of his own
time.

At best, his prayer for a simple life and a healthy and honored
old age is only competently done. Speaking in the third person as
"the poet," he prays:

> Grant him, kind heaven, the sum of his desires,
> What nature, not what luxury requires;

and,

> Let him in strength of mind and body live,
> But not his reason, nor his sense survive.

Of the Roman satirists, however, it is Juvenal, as has been asserted
repeatedly in this study, that served as Oldham's favorite model.
After all, Oldham came to be known to his contemporaries and to
posterity as the English Juvenal. It is not surprising that a poet of
his temperament, well schooled in the Roman classics, would turn
to the famous third satire for the subject of an imitation, *A Satire,
in Imitation of Juvenal* (1682). The parallels between Silver Age
Rome, crowded, noisy, dirty, full of foul smells, teeming with foreign-
ers, and Restoration London were irresistible. (In the next century,
Johnson imitated the same satire masterfully in his *London*.) The
Roman satirist's crusty old friend Umbricius informs him that, as an
honest citizen, he has no choice but to flee a corrupt city where
only liars, cheats, and flatterers flourish, where the clever Greek
prospers by fawning on the wealthy, where to be poor is to be a
figure of fun, where the streets pose a constant danger to life and
limb from both footpads and wayward chamber pots emptied into
narrow streets from upstairs windows. Where can one go but to a
rural retreat to live in peace and decency?

As the summary of its complaint makes clear, Juvenal's third
satire is read and translated with pleasure nowadays. The evils at-

tacked strike home for anyone who lives in the midst of today's metropolitan horrors. No matter how generalized Oldham's imitation may have seemed to readers of his time, it must have had an up-to-the-minute ring. The London of the 1680s was like the New York and London of our own time in that it was overrun by hordes of upstarts and opportunists in pursuit of the main chance—

> ... who once were grooms and footboys known,
> Are now to fair estates and honours grown....

As the Roman poet complained bitterly of the "Greeklings" who infested Rome, Oldham decries the French who filled the streets of Restoration London:

> A needy monsieur can be what he pleases,
> Groom, page, valet, quack, operator, fencer,
> Perfumer, pimp, Jack-pudding, juggler, dancer.

Throughout his rendition Oldham adds an air of freshness by alluding to characters notorious in the London of the time for either foolishness or nefariousness. His own neediness adds real feeling to his lines about the disgrace of being poor in a big city where men are judged on their wealth and display:

> 'Tis hard for any man to rise, that feels
> His virtue clogged with poverty at heels.

Like the Psalmist of old and the just man of any age, he is perplexed and moved to indignant eloquence at the spectacle of the prosperity of the unworthy, while he himself smarts from the pinch of poverty. The original Latin satire has several lines that stick in the memory, scathing lines describing how poverty makes even the worthiest of men cut ridiculous figures. Galled, undoubtedly, by his own poverty, Oldham renders them with economy of phrase and bite:

> Nothing in poverty so ill is borne,
> As its exposing men to grinning scorn.

The same passage also caused Johnson to rise to the occasion nobly, when he rendered it in equally bitter terms:

All crimes are safe, but hated poverty.

The curious reader need only turn again to the pages of Beljame's
Men of Letters and the English Public in the Eighteenth Century
to learn of the wretched plight of the writer in the late seventeenth
and eighteenth centuries. The livelihood of a poet in Silver Age Rome,
when a patron was also his only salvation, can only have been just as
precarious. It is easy to see why in Oldham's hands Juvenal's *Third
Satire* became much more than a college exercise.

It is noteworthy that James Boswell singled out Oldham's imitation as a worthy precursor of Johnson's *London.* Interestingly enough,
even though he speaks of the "many prosaick verses and bad rhymes"
in Oldham's version, as well as one error in translation, he concedes
that a passage in the original telling how the most difficult aspect of
poverty is that it makes men ridiculous is "better transfused" by
Oldham than by Johnson. The lines in question from the latter's
version read:

> Of all the griefs that harass the distrest,
> Sure the most bitter is a scornful jest.

According to Boswell, the matching lines in Oldham, already cited
above, are less elegant but more "just":

> Nothing in poverty so ill is borne,
> As its exposing men to grinning scorn.[12]

All in all, Oldham's performance with the *Third Satire* of Juvenal
is a creditable one, making up in vigor and genuine feeling what it
lacks in finesse.

Juvenal's *Third Satire* is not marked by a philosophic acceptance
of the evils of life. Nor was philosophic resignation ever one of
Oldham's strong points. Thus, he is much less successful in his
imitation of the same poet's *Thirteenth Satire* (*The Thirteenth Satire
of Juvenal, Imitated* (1682) and is unable to find a suitable English
equivalent of the stoic attitude with which the Roman poet consoles
a friend who has just been bilked of a sum of money by a deceitful
scoundrel. Dishonesty, Juvenal concludes cynically, is the norm in
everyday affairs, rather than a departure from the usual standard of
conduct. Only the naive expect honest behavior from their fellow-

men. The world is running down, continues the argument of the
satire, and the rugged virtues of earlier and happier eras have disappeared. For the man of true philosophic bent, the important thing
is that, no matter how corrupt the courts and how common perjury
and false witness, there is still that stern judge within everyone that
will punish him for his transgressions—his conscience.

The original, unfortunately, afforded Oldham insufficient material
for what he could do best, that is, turn a stream of invective on a
foe. While the tone of the original is resigned and reflective, Oldham's
diction and verse are inappropriately rough and unpolished, ill suited
to the task of conveying a melancholy world-weariness. Further, the
original offers an imitator few opportunities for topical digression
and acid commentary on contemporary figures and stylish vices.
As a result, Oldham's imitation must be considered a somewhat pedestrian exercise, of little interest as an independent work. The following
passage, detailing the punishing effects of conscience on "every villain
. . . that dares . . . be faithless, base, and false," is a sampling of the
best this imitation has to offer:

> Pale horror, ghastly fear, and black despair
> Pursue his steps, and dog him wheresoe'er
> He goes, and if from his loathed self he fly,
> To herd, like wounded deer, in company,
> These straight creep in and pall his mirth and joy,
>
> .   .   .
>
> Even wine, the greatest blessing of mankind,
> The best support of the dejected mind,
> Applied to his dull spirits, warms no more
> Than to his corpse it could past life restore.
> Darkness he fears, nor dares he trust his bed
> Without a candle watching by his side;
> And if the wakeful troubles of his breast
> To his tossed limbs allow one moment's rest,
> Straightways the groans of ghosts, and hideous screams
> Of tortured spirits, haunt his frightful dreams;
> Straight then returns to his tormented mind
> His perjured act, his injured God, and friend;
> Straight he imagines you before his eyes,
> Ghastly of shape, and of prodigious size,
> With glaring eyes, cleft foot, and monstrous tail
>
> .   .   .

Then starting wakes, and with a dismal cry,
Calls to his aid his frightened family;
There he owns the crime, and vows upon his knees
The sacred pledge next morning to release.

The scene depicted calls up memories of Elizabethan and Jacobean tragedies, of which Oldham, whose imagination ran to the outlandish and horrendous, must surely have been fond.

Imitations of Boileau

One of Oldham's most successful imitations is neither Horatian nor Juvenalian. It is his imitation of Boileau's *Eighth Satire* (1663), *The Eighth Satire of Monsieur Boileau, Imitated*, which he composed in 1682, a productive year in his career. The French poet held a special appeal for Oldham, as he did for writers of mock-heroic forms from Dryden's time well on into the Augustan age. Boileau's *Le Lutrin*, a mock-heroic treatment of a silly squabble of the canons of Sainte Chapelle in Paris, was a much-admired model. Professor Brooks suggests that a translation of the first canto of this work contained in the Bodleian Library, "The Desk, an Heroique Poem. First Canto," may be the work of Oldham.[13] But as for Boileau's *Eighth Satire*, it should be noted that it served as a model for one of the Earl of Rochester's finest poems, *A Satire Against Mankind*, a transcript of which in Oldham's own hand is to be found among his poems and drafts in the Bodleian MS.

The theme of the satire is a recurrent one in sixteenth- and seventeenth-century thought: the vanity and conceit of the puffed-up creature man who assigns himself so important a place in the universe. The theme was treated memorably by Montaigne in his *Apology for Raymond Sebond*. In a well-known passage the skeptical Montaigne writes:

Of all creatures man is the most miserable and fraile, and therewithall the proudest and disdainfullest. Who perceiveth and seeth himself placed here, amidst their filth and mire of the world, most senseless, and drooping part of the world, in the vilest corner of the house, and farthest from heavens coape, with those creatures, that are the worst of the three conditions; and yet dareth imaginarily place himselfe above the circle of the Moone, and reduce heaven under his feete. It is through the vanity of the same imagination, that he dare equall himselfe to God, that he ascribeth divine conditions unto himselfe, that he selecteth and separateth himself from out the ranke of other creatures; to which his fellow-brethren and compeers, he cuts out and shareth their parts, and allotteth them what portions of means or forces he thinkes good.[14]

As someone whose view of human nature was always that of the satirist, Oldham had no difficulty accepting the view expressed in the passage just quoted, and is willing to entertain the notion that a beast can be regarded as superior to a man, once man is seen from the standpoint of the beast. Lovers of Montaigne remember the passage in the same essay in which he raises an intriguing question about his cat:

When I am playing with my Cat, who knowes whether she have more sport in dallying with me, than I have in gaming with her?

Such salutary deflating of swollen little man and such comparing him to his disfavor with what he regards as the lower orders are an old occupation of philosophers and are to be found in Plato and Plutarch, among the great writers of antiquity.

The setting of the satire is a university disputation—a happy stroke, since no setting could show man more pompous and puffed up with the sense of his own importance. As is frequently the case in Horace and Juvenal, the satire is a quasi-dramatic monologue. The poet, speaking directly, rebuts the arguments raised by a doctor of the university; thus, the doctor's contentions are reported only indirectly to the reader. When the poet asserts that "Of all the creatures in the world that be," "the arrantest fool" is man, the doctor is outraged. How, he asks, can anyone seriously dispute man's position at the very summit of creation?

> 'Man is' . . . 'Lord of the Universe';
> For him was the fair frame of nature made,
> And all the creatures for his use and aid;
> To him alone, of all the living kind,
> Has bounteous Heaven the reasoning gift assigned.

True enough, the poet agrees, reason has been granted to man, but man uses the faculty so rarely as to make himself contemptible. And what about wisdom, which the "grave doctors" call

> an evenness of soul,
> A steady temper, which no cares control,
> No passions ruffle, nor desires inflame? ...

How often do men achieve this Stoic serenity? Or any other virtues?
Think for just a moment, the poet argues, of the beasts in connection
with man's supposed superiority. Are men, for example, as provident
as the lowly ant? Are any creatures as fickle and inconstant as men—

> That foolish, fickle, motley creature, man,
> More changing than a weathercock....

Indeed,

> This titular king, who thus pretends to be
> Lord of all, how many lords has he?

He is, the poet reminds us, the slave of his own passions—notably
avarice and lust for power. But there is no need to rehearse the list of
passions as they are found in the seventeenth-century moral treatises.
Only examine man in what he himself thinks is his best light: as
a member of a social and political body subject to law. How quickly
this glorious light fades away when we remind ourselves how often
and viciously men cheat and plunder their fellowmen—often under
the cloak of legality—and wage war on other societies.

The burden of the argument, as readers of Horace and Montaigne
are aware, is a familiar, even hackneyed one. But Oldham imparts
to his imitation the fiercely indignant tone so characteristic of him
whenever he reflects on living in a society in which

> He that is rich, is everything that is.

As for that much-vaunted human reason, this faculty only proves
to be a curse for many men, especially for fools who persist in delud-
ing themselves as to their capacities and talents. How wise, on the
other hand, the animal who calmly follows his instincts and does
not set up for a "vain ass of parts." Certainly the animal never debases
himself as do self-appointed men of parts. Familiarizing his model,
Oldham tells his readers that a jeered-at ass would jeer at men if
he were forced to stand for an hour in Fleet Street or the Strand

and observe the "two-legged herd" of vain, pompous, pettifogging men in all their various disguises.

Oldham expands Boileau's three hundred or so lines to more than four hundred of his own. Even so, he sticks close to his model, at the expense at times of losing freshness and vigor of expression. Sometimes he is overly literal and even seems to try to replicate the cadence and syntax of the original French, as when he renders the opening lines ("De tous les animaux qui s'elevant dans l'air") this way:

Of all the creatures in the world...

On several occasions he even echoes some of Boileau's rhymes.

Thus, his effort does not fare well when, as is inevitable, it is compared with Rochester's *Satire Against Mankind*, an earlier imitation (ca. 1674) of the same model. We have already noted that Oldham was well acquainted with this version, having transcribed it in his own hand under the title *Satyr Upon Man*. Although Johnson in his life of Rochester remarks curtly that Rochester can "only claim what remains when all of Boileau's part is taken away," his rendering of the satire, literal though it may be, captures the philosophic tone of the original's condemnation of man's foolishness and depravity. Above all, Rochester's verses are gracefully turned. Besides, Johnson's complaint about his over-reliance on the original is exaggerated. He did not follow Boileau as closely as did Oldham. Rather, he adapted to his own uses the common store of ideas inherited from Hobbes, Montaigne, and the whole tradition of thought about man's flawed nature that underlie the satire. The result is an original and justly celebrated poem.

But to return to Oldham and his use of Boileau as a source: he also imitated another of the French poet's satires in *A Satire Touching Nobility*, which must be counted among his more successful imitations, its success due, in part, to his finding the subject particularly congenial. Bell in a note in his edition of Oldham points to this imitation as having influenced Pope. The latter's indebtedness to Oldham, he says,

may easily be determined by a comparison between this fluent and spirited version of one of Boileau's Satires and the Fourth Epistle of the Essay on Man.[15]

Bell's statement, of course, must be tempered by the reader's realization that the theme, the disappearance of true nobility from society, was a favorite one stemming from the classical writers of antiquity. The satire opposes true nobility, based on virtue, honor, and care for the weak, to self-indulgence, trading on the fame of ancestors, and vain concern with the mere trappings of nobility: the coats of arms, the equipage, the ceremonies. No one can ever mistake genuine nobility, for

> Virtue's the certain mark, by Heaven designed,
> That's always stamped upon a noble mind.

When he looks around at the dissipated and useless progeny of noble lines, Oldham warms up to his theme:

> Cursed be the day, when first this vanity
> Did primitive simplicity destroy
>
>   .   .   .
>
> When glory sprung from innocence alone;
> Each from his merit only title drew,
> And that alone made kings, and nobles too.

If one looks hard enough, it is true, as Bell argues, he can find similarities of idea between passages of the *Satire Touching Nobility* and the *Essay on Man*. But one would be hard pressed to turn up similarities of language indicating that Pope was influenced directly by Oldham's adaptation. The simple fact is that Boileau, Rochester, Oldham, and Pope were all drawing upon an inherited stock of ideas, the principal among them, such as the notion that worth and happiness reside in the conscious exercise of virtue, to be found in Aristotle's *Ethics* and the ancient philosophers.

Oldham's Achievement as an Imitator

Oldham, on the whole, seldom produced what, paradoxically, can be thought of as "original" imitations, as did Dryden, Pope, and Johnson. Dryden in a well-known passage in his preface to his translation of Ovid's *Epistles* (1680), a statement Oldham must have pondered, distinguished among the kinds of "translations":

All translation may be reduced to these three heads. First that of metaphrase, or turning an author word by word, and line by line, from one language into another. ... the second way is that of paraphrase, or translation with latitude, where the author is kept in view by the translator, so as never to be lost, but his words are not so strictly followed as his sense. ... The third way is that of imitation, where the translator (if now he has not lost that name) assumes the liberty, not only to vary from the words and sense, but to forsake them both as he sees occasion; and taking only some general hints from the original, to run division on the ground works, as he pleases.

Later, in the *Dedication of the Aeneis* (1697), Dryden describes how he "had long considered that the way to please the best judges is not to translate a poet literally":

On the whole matter, I thought fit to steer betwixt the two extremes of paraphrase and literal translation; to keep as near my author as I could, without losing all his graces, the most eminent of which are in the beauty of his words. ...

In the course of summing up the art of translation, he expresses neatly and pithily the secret of the successful "imitation" of an author:

I have endeavoured to make Virgil speak such English as he would himself have spoken if he had been born in England and in this present age.[16]

As an imitator of writers of generalized satire, Oldham has earned a secure place for himself in literary history as a talented innovator, someone who could point to correspondences between life in ancient Rome and life in Restoration England. In fact, his position as a practitioner, or, more accurately, a forerunner, of the art of imitation involves a certain irony in that it was earned at the cost of what he really aspired to achieve as a writer, a place in the London literary scene. There is much insight in C. W. Previté-Orton's comments in the *Cambridge History of English Literature* to the effect that the very life Oldham loathed, that of an obscure schoolmaster in a remote village, helped make him—ironically enough—the forerunner in imitation of figures like Pope and Johnson:

... the aloofness of his life from the capital, combined with the classical studies necessary for his occupation, was a fit environment for the first author of generalizing satires, where incidental railing gives place to artistic composition without too constant a reference to immediate facts.[17]

If we take Dryden's scheme of the kinds of translation and his own achievements in translation as touchstones, we must award Oldham a place as a talented master of paraphrase, one who learned to render a source with "latitude." On occasion, as in his version of Horace's *Ninth Satire of the First Book*, he rises to the level of imitation as Dryden defined it.

Chapter Five

A View of His Reputation

His Early Reputation

We have seen in this study how Oldham earned the respect of his contemporaries as a poet and scholar. Unfortunately, his reputation was short-lived, lasting only into the century after his death. Brooks in his *Bibliography* notes that he influenced directly a line of minor writers for over a generation, numbering among his followers now forgotten figures like Thomas Wood, Robert Gould, Thomas Andrews, and the notorious Grub Street author "Tom" Brown. Brooks asserts, in fact, that this influence was considerable:

From their first appearance until the early years of the eighteenth century his poems affected the current verse of the day, the anonymous content of broadside, pamphlet, and miscellany.[1]

In fact, Dryden's own version of Juvenal's *Third Satire* seems to owe something to Oldham. Major writers of the next century, like Swift, Prior, Steele, and Congreve were acquainted with his work. Boswell tells us that Johnson even thought of editing his poems.

We also noted in a preceding chapter that when he was a boy of twelve, Alexander Pope bought a copy of a 1692 edition of Oldham's works, a copy which passed into the possession of Edward Thompson, the editor of the 1770 collection. The young Pope annotated certain passages and listed what he considered the best works on a flyleaf. Professor Brooks describes for us the manuscript notes on the flyleaves at the beginning and end of the book, which is now in the British Museum. The beginning leaf contains the following history of the wanderings of this copy, for which Pope paid four shillings:

E Libris Alexandri Pope; Pret. 4 s 1700 Sept. 23 1768 given unto Edw. Thompson in the King's Bench prison by John Wilkes this volume came from Mr. Pope & the remarks are in his own hand writing in the last page.[2]

The leaf, regarded as really being inscribed in Pope's own hand, lists "The most Remarkable Works in this Author, as follow Here: Fourth Satire on the Jesuits, Satire on Virtue, The Translation of Horace's Art of Poetry, The Impertinent, from Horace Satire 9, Book 1, and To the Memory of Mr. Charles Morwent." But, it should be noted, as also indicated earlier, that Joseph Spence in his *Anecdotes, Observations, and Characteristics of Books and Men* reports that Pope eventually came to regard Oldham as a "very indelicate writer," whose rage was strong but "too much like Billingsgate."[3]

Oldham, as we have seen, won the acclaim of contemporaries and critics in the century after his death as a translator and imitator, as well as a satirist. Even John Dennis, who carried on a bitter feud with Pope because of the latter's lack of passion, conceded his "wit" and "genius" as a translator. We have also already noted that this same stern judge, who himself translated the tale of Byblis from the *Metamorphoses*, singled out Oldham's translation of the same episode for praise, qualified though it was. Again, the high regard in which Samuel Johnson held Oldham bears repeating. We must credit Oldham, he tells us, along with Rochester, with having developed a "kind of middle composition between translation and original design." The Warton brothers, Joseph and Thomas, also held Oldham in critical esteem, the former, in his *Essay on the Genius and Writing of Pope* (1756), ranking him along with Butler, Swift, Rochester, Donne, and Dorset as one of the "men of wit, of elegant taste, and lively fancy. . . ." Thomas Warton, in his *History of English Poetry*, published in the last quarter of the eighteenth century, also placed Oldham in the company of Rochester and Pope as an outstanding practitioner of the art of imitating the ancients.

Along with his acknowledged merit as a writer of imitations, Oldham achieved standing in his own time as an original satirist. "A Short Essay on English Satire," gathered in 1764 in the *Works of Tom Brown*, lists him, with Rochester and Dorset, as one of "the greatest Satirists of the English." According to the essayist, he is like Juvenal in his rage, but, like the same Roman poet, is given to excess. Yet, these faults of excess notwithstanding, "he was born a poet. . . ."[4]

For contemporary and later critics, likening Oldham to Juvenal became customary, particularly in view of the success of the *Satires Upon the Jesuits*, short-lived though it was. For example, the notice of the poet in the Reverend James Granger's *A Biographical History of England* (first ed., 1769) asserts that the *Satires Upon the Jesuits* gained him the appellation of the English Juvenal, as they have much of the indignant spirit and manner of the Roman poet.[5]

Alexander Chalmers in his *General Biographical Dictionary* (1812) concurs in the "appellation," repeating that the attack on the Jesuits "procured him the title of the English Juvenal."[6] The book collector and bibliographer Robert Watt laconically confirms Oldham's reputation as a satirist in his own generation when in his *Bibliotheca Britannica* (1824), after listing his works, he comments: "By these he acquired great fame."

Oldham gained the respect, as well as the critical esteem, of contemporaries. Reprinted in Edward Thompson's 1770 edition of his works, *Compositions in Prose and Verse of Mr. John Oldham* (vol. 1) are a number of memorial verses, all of which commend him as a satirist and praise him for lashing out at the vices of the age.

Present Status of His Reputation

Although the anthologists either ignore him entirely or give him little space, most of the historians of English literature have some words of praise for Oldham. A. W. Ward, contributor of the article on the poet to the *Dictionary of National Biography* (vol. 14), reflects the judgment of most historians and critics when he concludes:

Oldham's productions deserve more notice than they have received. Their own original power is notable. Pope, and perhaps others of the chief eighteenth-century poets, were under obligation to their author.

It would be foolhardy, however, to anticipate a serious revival of interest in Oldham's works. Although his deserves to be an enduring voice, the subjects of his polemic and the objects of his vigorous attacks have long since been relegated to the mustier pages of history. Only the freshness of his adaptations of other writers, Juvenal in particular, and the raw bite of his *Satires Upon the Jesuits* can hold appeal for a modern reader whose interests are other than antiquarian. His onslaught against the Jesuits, no matter how excessive the abuse and frenzied the tone, still has an authentic Juvenalian sting.

As a result of the efforts of Professor Brooks and the timely appearance of Yale *POAS* II, Oldham's work may undergo a revaluation, especially if the modern edition of the canon of his work that

Brooks has promised us appears. We have already noted how the
Times Literary Supplement reviewer of the Yale *POAS* II, (Nov. 25,
1965), in which is published for the first time an up-to-date annotated edition of the *Satires Upon the Jesuits*, suggests that the time
has come to restore Oldham to his rightful place in Restoration
literature:

One can see the justice of Dryden's . . . claims in the moving elegy on his
"too little and too lately known young friend," and the appearance here
of the first modern edition of Oldham's major work may well, as Professor
Mengel says, lead to a revaluation of him.

Professor Mengel, the editor of Yale *POAS* II, expresses hope that
this first modern edition of Oldham's major work,

set in . . . historical context, may help to show what Dryden found to
praise in him and why his reputation ran so high during his brief career.[7]

Now that the Yale edition of *POAS* has made the satiric forms
and conventions in which the times abounded more easily accessible
to modern students, the rightness of Rachel Trickett's and George
deF. Lord's remarks that Dryden cannot be considered a school unto
himself becomes more apparent. Over the years, the notion of Dryden
as opening, working, and exhausting a vein of satire—for example,
imitations designed to deplore the conditions under which writers
had to work, epistles on social matters, town eclogues, the Horatian
satire—has become well established. David Vieth and other scholars
are now demonstrating that Oldham and Rochester were also masters
of these forms. Many of the conventions, as found in *POAS* and other
collections, were short-lived and faddish; for example, the popular
instructions to a painter in which an apparition appears to warn
or counsel against impending doom, as in Marvell's *Last Instructions
to a Painter*, or in Oldham's *Satire Concerning Poetry*, in which the
ghost of Spenser appears. Someone like Pope, Trickett asserts, looked
"for more permanent conventions" in earlier satirists:

He found much of value in the poems of Oldham and Rochester, for these
two poets had caught most of the contemporary attitudes and wrote with
all the contemporary vigour. And each of them did so in a detached and
independent fashion which showed how a poet with no particular political
allegiance could make good use of topical materials.

Oldham was a pioneer in replacing the musty types of satire with real people, a practice which reached a state of perfection in Pope's *Moral Epistles.* Trickett credits Oldham with a signal achievement. He made "the imitation a formal excuse for satire which was free of the stigma of party journalism."[8]

Whether the work that brought Oldham the greatest fame during his own lifetime, the *Satires Upon the Jesuits*, will ever attract the widespread attention of modern scholars, is questionable, unless they read them with pleasure as original and ingenious adaptations of Juvenalian vigor for the purpose of excoriating a public enemy. But there can be no doubt that Oldham deserves wider recognition, if not as an innovator, then as a significant pioneer in establishing the imitation as a literary genre. Any student of the Restoration who reads this satirist whose work was prized by his contemporaries will agree that he succeeded in accomplishing, to some degree, what Dryden urged in the preface to his own version of Ovid's *Epistles*:

I take imitation of an author ... to be an endeavour of a later poet to write like one who has written before him, on the same subject; that is, not to translate his words or to be confined in his sense, but only to set him as a pattern, and to write as he supposes that author would have done, had he lived in our age, and in our country.

This describes a goal Oldham came close to achieving.

The estimate of James Sutherland and others of Oldham as one of the "primitives" in the development of English satire is a fair one. He never reached the level of great and enduring satire because he specialized in abuse too much for its own sake. Thus, as satire, his work is a cut below that of satirists whose purpose is to castigate so as to reform and make men laugh at their own follies. As Sutherland reminds us:

Behind the satire of Juvenal and Swift and Pope, of Voltaire and Shaw, there lies some vision of good life, of order and decency, of good sense and moderation, of intelligence and spiritual alertness.[9]

When compared with the satirists named by Sutherland, Oldham can seem callow and without depth. His interests were too parochial, his experience too narrow, his life too short and embittered to have given him the "vision" that might have imparted to his attacks on human folly and malice a truly universal quality.

Professor Brooks, who has contributed so much to the revaluation of Oldham, should be allowed his final word. He sums up well the poet's achievement in a short lifetime and places it within the history of English literature:

As a practitioner of various genres, and in those of the Augustan 'Imitation' and of heroic satire an important contributor to the form they afterwards assumed in the hands of major poets, he is significant to the historian of literature. For the social historian, he has a wealth of topical allusion and description: moreover, he both discusses the social position of the man of letters and exemplifies it in his own career and in the poems by which he hoped that career might be furthered.[10]

There can be no more fitting way to bring this study of a neglected writer to a close than to quote Dryden's "To the Memory of Mr. Oldham," an encomium that gently assesses the young poet's strengths and weaknesses:

> Farewel, too little and too lately known,
> Whom I began to think and call my own;
> For sure our Souls were near ally'd, and thine
> Cast in the same poetick mould with mine.
> One common note on either Lyre did strike,
> And Knaves and Fools we both abhorr'd alike:
> To the same Goal did both our studies drive,
> The last set out the soonest did arrive.
> Thus *Nisus* fell upon the slippery place,
> While his young Friend perform'd and won the Race.
> O early ripe! to thy abundant store
> What could advancing Age have added more?
> It might (what Nature never gives the young)
> Have taught the numbers of thy native Tongue.
> But Satyr needs not those, and Wit will shine
> Through the harsh cadence of a rugged line.
> A noble Error, and but seldom made,
> When Poets are by too much force betray'd.
> Thy generous fruits, though gather'd ere their prime
> Still shew'd a quickness; and maturing time
> But mellows what we write to the dull sweets of Rime.
> Once more, hail and farewel; farewel, thou young,
> But ah too short, *Marcellus* of our tongue;
> Thy Brows with Ivy, and with Laurels bound;
> But Fate and gloomy Night encompass thee around.

Notes and References

Chapter One

1. *The Poems of John Oldham*, ed. Robert Bell, introduction by Bonamy Dobrée, Centaur Classics (Carbondale, Ill., 1960), p. 5. Hereafter referred to as *Poems*.
2. *Athenae Oxonienses*, ed. Philip Bliss (London, 1820), 4:119. Hereafter referred to as *A. O.*
3. These manuscripts and others in the British Museum are described in Harold F. Brooks, *A Bibliography of John Oldham*, Proceedings and Papers of the Oxford Bibliographical Society, V, pt. L, 1936, 10ff. Hereafter referred to as *Bibliography*.
4. Ibid., p. 5.
5. "The Poems of John Oldham," in *Restoration Literature*, ed. Harold Love (London, 1972), p. 181. Hereafter referred to as Brooks.
6. *A. O.*, 4:119.
7. Brooks, p. 178.
8. A. Beljame, *Men of Letters and the English Public in the Eighteenth Century* (London, 1948), p. 122.
9. *Poems*, note, p. 43.
10. Ibid., note, p. 10.
11. Brooks, p. 179.
12. Ibid., p. 178.
13. *Bibliography*, entry 1, 10.
14. See Brooks, n. 4, p. 200.
15. David Vieth, *The Complete Poems of John Wilmot Earl of Rochester* (New Haven, 1968), p. xxvii.
16. *A. O.*, 4:119.
17. Brooks, p. 180.
18. Rachel Trickett, *The Honest Muse* (Oxford, 1967), p. 90.
19. Johann Prinz, *John Wilmot Earl of Rochester* (Leipzig: Mayer and Müller, 1927), p. 89.
20. Brooks, p. 183.
21. Beljame, *Men of Letters and the English Public in the Eighteenth Century*, p. 130.
22. Brooks, p. 182.

Chapter Two

1. See "John Oldham, the Wits, and a Satyr Against Virtue," *Philological Quarterly* 32 (1954):90–93.
2. *Bibliography*, entry 15, p. 25.
3. *A. O.*, 4:120.
4. Brooks, p. 190.
5. *Poems*, n. p. 238.
6. Ibid., n. p. 50.
7. W. J. Courthope, *History of English Poetry* (New York, 1962), 3:498.

Chapter Three

1. Maurice Ashley, *England in the Seventeenth Century*, No. 6 in the "Pelican History of England" (Baltimore, 1961), p. 136.
2. Ibid., p. 140.
3. *History of My Own Time*, ed. O. Airy (Oxford, 1897), 2:200.
4. *Character of a Tory*, in *Somers Tracts* (1750), pt. II, 3:282; *Character of a Protestant Jesuit*, in Bodleian Ashmore G. 12. Both quoted in *Poems on Affairs of State*, ed. Elias F. Mengel, Jr. (New Haven, 1965), 2:xxiv and xxv. Hereafter this work is referred to as Yale *POAS* II.
5. See Narcissus Luttrell, *Brief Historical Relation of State Affairs from September 1678 to April 1714*, 6 vols. (Oxford, 1857); Sir John Dalrymple, *Memoirs of Great Britain and Ireland from the Dissolution of the last Parliament of Charles till the Dissolution of the French and Spanish Fleets at Vigo*, 2d ed. (London: W. Strahan and T. Cadell, 1771).
6. Reprinted in Yale *POAS* I, ed. George deF. Lord.
7. Ibid., p. xxv.
8. C. V. Wedgewood, *Poetry and Politics Under the Stuarts* (Cambridge, 1961), pp. 138, 143.
9. See Yale *POAS* I, p. 190.
10. Yale *POAS* II, p. 215: for full text see pp. 209–16.
11. *The Life and Times of Anthony Wood*, ed. Andrew Clark (Oxford, 1894), 2:422.
12. *Citt and Bumpkin* (1680); reprinted by Augustan Reprint Society, University of California at Los Angeles, 1965, No. 117, p. 7.
13. Jane Lane, *Titus Oates* (London, 1949), p. 40.
14. All references to *Absalom and Achitophel* are to the text as reprinted in Yale *POAS* II, pp. 455–93.
15. G. W. Keeton, *Lord Chancellor Jeffreys and the Stuart Cause* (London: Macdonald, 1965), p. 83.
16. Luttrell, *Brief Relation*, 1:5.

17. Quoted in William Sachse, *English History in the Making* (New York: Xerox College Publishing, 1967), 1:294.

18. Burnet, *History of My Own Time*, 2:179.

19. Ibid., p. 229.

20. "Anonymous Account of the Popish Plot," October 31, 1678, in *English Historical Documents*, ed. Andrew Browning (New York: Oxford University Press, 1953), 8:105–9.

21. Richard Duke, "A Panegyric Upon Oates," 1679, in Yale *POAS* II, pp. 127–30.

22. See Luttrell's *Popish Plot Catalogue*, Introduction by F. C. Francis (Oxford, 1956).

23. Dalrymple, *Memoirs of Great Britain and Ireland*, 2:43.

24. See J. G. Muddiman, *The King's Journalist* (London, 1923), p. 210.

25. John Pollock, *The Popish Plot* (London, 1903), p. 64.

26. Ashley, *England in the Seventeenth Century*, pp. 243–44.

27. "Truth Brought to Light or Murder Will Out" (1679), *POAS* II, p. 14.

28. Brooks, p. 180.

29. James Sutherland, *English Literature of the Late Seventeenth Century* (Oxford, 1969), p. 165.

30. James Sutherland, *English Satire* (Cambridge, 1958), p. 36.

31. Ibid., p. 38.

32. Brooks, p. 180.

33. See "The Genesis of John Oldham's *Satyrs Upon the Jesuits, PMLA* 58 (1934):958–70.

34. See "Influence of Ben Jonson's *Catiline* upon John Oldham's *Satyrs Upon the Jesuits, ELH* 11 (1944):38–62.

35. See Ruth Nevo, *Dial of Virtue* (Princeton, 1963), pp. 8ff.

36. Mark Van Doren, *John Dryden*, reprinted as A Midland Book (Bloomington, Ind., 1967), p. 146.

37. Roger Sharrock, "Modes of Satire," in *Restoration Theatre*, ed. J. R. Brown and B. Harris, Stratford-upon-Avon Studies, 1965, 6:120, 123.

38. Trickett, *The Honest Muse*, p. 94.

39. Sutherland, *English Satire*, p. 47.

Chapter Four

1. Vieth, *Complete Poems of John Wilmot Earl of Rochester*, headnote, p. 120.

2. Harold Love, *Restoration Literature*, p. 149.

3. Sutherland, *English Literature of the Late Seventeenth Century*, p. 166.

4. *Poems of Alexander Pope* ("Imitations of Horace"), ed. John Butt (London and New Haven: Yale University Press, 1961), 4:xxvi.

5. See *Bibliography*, entry 7, p. 12.

6. Samuel Johnson, *Lives of the Poets*, Oxford World Classics, 2:294.

7. Brooks, p. 195.

8. Ibid., p. 185.

9. See *The Poems*, n., p. 21.

10. See Harold F. Brooks, "The 'Imitation' in English Poetry," *Review of English Studies* 25 (1949):124–40.

11. Sutherland, *English Literature of the Seventeenth Century*, p. 116.

12. See Boswell's *Life of Johnson*, ed. G. B. Hill, rev. L. F. Powell (Oxford: Clarendon Press, 1934), 1:118–20; for Johnson's planned edition of Oldham's works see n. 1, 4:381.

13. See *Bibliography*, entry 40, p. 37, for a description of 1712 translation of Boileau's works "made English"; also see the introduction to *Le Lutrin*, Augustan Reprint Society, No. 126, p. 11.

14. See *The Essayes of Montaigne*, trans. John Florio, in Everyman's Library edition, 2:142.

15. *Poems*, n., p. 215.

16. See *Essays of John Dryden*, vols. 1 and 2, ed. W. Ker (New York: Russell and Russell, 1961).

17. C. W. Previté-Orton, "Political and Ecclesiastical Satire," *CHEL*, 8:83–84.

Chapter Five

1. *Bibliography*, p. 7.

2. Ibid., entry 23, 28. Entries describe Alexander Pope's copy of Oldham's *Works*, which is a composite of the editions of 1685 and 1695. The notations are regarded by authorities as being in Pope's own hand.

3. Joseph Spence, *Anecdotes, Observations, and Characteristics of Books and Men*, ed. James Osborne (Oxford: Clarendon Press, 1966), 2:274.

4. See *Works*, 9th ed. (London, 1784), 1:27–28.

5. James Granger, *A Biographical History of England*, 5th ed. (London: William Baynes, 1824).

6. See Alexander Chalmers, *General Biographical Dictionary*, new and enlarged ed. (London: J. Nichols *et al.*, 1815), 32:330–331.

7. Yale *POAS* II, p. xxxii.

8. Trickett, *The Honest Muse*, p. 104.

9. Sutherland, *English Satire*, p. 42.

10. Brooks, p. 177.

Selected Bibliography

PRIMARY SOURCES

1. Bibliography and Textual Study

Brooks, Harold F. *A Bibliography of John Oldham*. Proceedings of the Oxford Bibliographical Society, V. Pt. i. Oxford: Oxford University Press, 1926. The forty-two bibliographical entries describe manuscripts, editions of separate works, collected works, works of others containing poems by Oldham—even an epigraph in Malmesbury Abbey churchyard thought to be one of the poet's earliest productions. Introduction supplies details of poet's life and an estimate of his standing as a poet and satirist.

————. *The Complete Works of John Oldham*. Abstract Diss., University of Oxford, 1940. In Abstracts of Dissertations, vol. 12. Oxford: Clarendon Press, 1940. Brooks prepared an edition of the works which has not yet been published. An informative commentary places Oldham in the development of "heroic satire" from *Hudibras* to *MacFlecknoe*.

2. Separate Works

Satyrs Upon the Jesuits . . . and some other pieces. Written in the year 1679. London: Printed for Joseph Hindmarsh, 1681.

Some New Pieces Never Before Published by the Author of the Satyrs Upon the Jesuits. London: Printed by M. C. for Joseph Hindmarsh, 1681.

Poems and Translations. London: Printed for Joseph Hindmarsh, 1683.

Satires Upon the Jesuits. In *Poems on Affairs of State*, vol. 2. New Haven: Yale University Press, 1965. Edited by Elias F. Mengel, Jr. This is the first modern, fully annotated edition of Oldham's *magnum opus*, a boon to the student of seventeenth-century satire.

3. Collected Works

The Works of Mr. John Oldham, Together with his Remains. London: Printed for Jo. Hindmarsh, 1684. Brooks describes copies of this edition which was substantively reissued by Hindmarsh in 1684, in 1686, and in 1692, as an indication of the demand for the poet's works.

The Works of Mr. John Oldham Together with his Remains. 2 vols. London: Printed by J. Bettenham for Dr. Brown, et al., 1722. This volume contains the anonymous memoir of the poet's life and some explanatory notes.

Compositions in Prose and Verse of Mr. John Oldham. To which are Added Memoirs of His life and Explanatory Notes Upon some Obscure Passages of his Writing. Edited by Edward Thompson. In three volumes. London: Printed for W. Flexney, 1770. There are notes by Thompson.

Poetical Works of John Oldham. London: John W. Parker, 1854; Reprint. Carbondale: Southern Illinois University Press, 1960. Edited by Robert Bell. Bell's edition, which was included in the inexpensive Annotated Edition of the English Poets, omits nineteen of the poems included in Thompson's edition above. The 1960 reprint in Centaur Classics contains an introductory essay of appreciation by Bonamy Dobrée.

SECONDARY SOURCES

1. Special Studies

Brooks, Harold F. "The 'Imitation' in English Poetry." *Review of English Studies* 25 (1949):124–40. Article traces the history of the "imitation" in English, with considerable attention to Oldham's achievement.

———. "The Poetry of John Oldham." In *Restoration Literature: Critical Approaches*, edited by Harold Love, pp. 177–203. London: Methuen, 1972. This is an indispensable essay which surveys and places in perspective the work of Oldham.

Cable, C. H. "Oldham's Borrowings from Buchanan." *Modern Language Notes* 66 (1951). This is useful to the student in the study of the third of the *Satires Upon the Jesuits.*

Mackin, C. R. "The Satiric Technique of Oldham's *Satyrs Upon the Jesuits.*" *Studies in Philology* 62 (1965).

Sharrock, Roger. "Modes of Satire." In *Restoration Theatre*, edited by J. R. Brown and B. Harris, pp. 109–35. *Stratford-upon-Avon Studies* 6, 1965.

Trickett, Rachel. *The Honest Muse.* Oxford: Clarendon Press, 1967. Chapter 4 ("The Conventions of Satire") is especially valuable in placing Oldham's satire within the conventions of the age. There is also valuable and enlightening discussion of Rochester's influence on Oldham and the latter's achievement in the art of the imitation.

Vieth, David M. "Oldham, The Wits and A Satyr Against Virtue." *Philo-*

logical Quarterly 32 (1953). This is a helpful discussion of the interesting question of Oldham's relations with people like Rochester, Sedley, and others of the Court Wits.

―――. *Attribution in Restoration Poetry*. New Haven: Yale University Press, 1963. This is a standard work in its field.

―――. *The Complete Poems of John Wilmot, Earl of Rochester*. New Haven: Yale University Press, 1968. The introduction and notes contain references to Oldham.

Williams, W. M. "The Genesis of John Oldham's *Satyrs Upon the Jesuits*." *PMLA* 57 (1943):958–70. Williams attempts to show that Oldham adopted forms of native political satire then current.

―――. "The Influence of Ben Jonson's *Catiline* Upon John Oldham's *Satyrs Upon the Jesuits*." *ELH* 11 (1944):38–62. This is a detailed comparison of *Catiline* with the four satires.

Wykes, D. "Aspects of Restoration Irony: John Oldham." *English Studies* 52 (1971):223–31.

―――. "Oldham and Phineas Fletcher: An Unrecognized Source for *Satyrs upon the Jesuits*." *Review of English Studies*, n.s. 12 (1971): 410–22, 23 (1972):19–34. This is a source study in two parts.

2. General Studies: Literary Background

Beljame, A. *Men of Letters and the English Public in the Eighteenth Century*. Edited, with introduction and notes by Bonamy Dobrée. Translated by E. O. Lorimer. London: Kegan Paul, 1948. Chapter 2 of this well-known and still useful study by a French scholar deals with "political literature" under Charles II and James I.

Garnett, R. *The Age of Dryden*. London: George Bell, 1903. See pp. 42–46 in particular.

Nevo, Ruth. *The Dial of Virtue*. Princeton, N.J.: Princeton University Press, 1963. There is some discussion of Oldham in course of study of seventeenth-century literature. See especially pp. 183–84.

Previté-Orton, C. W. "Political and Ecclesiastical Satire." In Volume 8, Chapter 3, of *Cambridge History of English Literature*. Author argues that with the Popish Plot political satire in England came into its own, with Oldham "the first poet who entered the lists."

Sutherland, James. *English Satire*. Cambridge: Cambridge University Press, 1958. Chapter 3 is of special interest to the student of Oldham, with attention given to "primitive" forms: invective and lampoon.

―――. *English Literature of the Late Seventeenth Century*. Vol. 6 in *Oxford History of English Literature*. New York: Oxford University Press, 1969. Oldham is discussed on pages 164–67. Sutherland argues that the Horatian imitations are the best realized of the works.

3. General Studies: Political and Social Background

Ashley, Maurice. *England in the Seventeenth Century.* (1603–1714) Vol.
6 in *The Pelican History of England.* Baltimore: Penguin Books,
1961. This is a brief and readable introduction to a period of great
ferment in all spheres of activity.

Burnet, Gilbert. *History of My Own Time.* 2 vols. Edited by Osmund
Airy. Oxford: Clarendon Press, 1897. The first volume of this was
published in 1724 and is valuable for first-hand accounts of the
frenzy surrounding the Popish Plot from someone who dismissed
Oates as a credible witness.

Carr, J. D. *The Murder of Sir Edmund Godfrey.* New York: Harper,
1936. Readable study of the baffling murder that helped fan the
flames of anti-Catholic feeling by a well-known writer of mysteries.

Case, A. E. *A Bibliography of English Poetical Miscellanies, 1521–1750.*
Oxford: The Bibliographical Society, 1935. This is an indispensable
reference tool of students of political satires and lampoons.

Courthope, W. J. *A History of English Poetry*, Vol. 3. New York: Russell
and Russell, 1962. Pages 498–502 contain a judicious assessment of
Oldham's achievement.

Chappell, W. and Ebsworth, J. W., eds. *The Roxburghe Ballads.* 9 vols.
(Hertford, 1871–97). Vol. 4 contains "various ballads and squibs
which mark the anti-papal disturbances of 1678–89. . . ."

Evelyn, John. *The Diary of John Evelyn.* Edited by E. S. de Beer. 6 vols.
Oxford: Clarendon Press, 1955. This diary, along with Pepys's better-
known one, is invaluable for students of the period.

Kenyon, John. *The Popish Plot.* London: Heinemann, 1972. This is a
thorough examination of the Plot and its fearful effects on both
Catholics and Protestants.

Lane, Jane. *Titus Oates.* London: Andrew Dakers, 1949. This is a modern
and well-written account of one of history's most villainous liars.

Lord, George deF., ed. *Poems on Affairs of State*, vol. 1. New Haven:
Yale University Press, 1963. Introduction is useful for the background
it provides of the political satire of the age. The Yale *POAS* series,
now complete, covers the period from 1660–1714.

Luttrell, Narcissus. *A Brief Historical Relation of State Affairs from September 1678 to April 1714.* 6 vols. Oxford: Oxford University Press,
1857. Macaulay brought the manuscript of this day-by-day chronicle
to the attention of readers in his *History of England*, whereupon it
was published. Luttrell was an extreme anti-papist.

————. *Narcissus Luttrell's Popist Plot Catalogue.* Edited by F. C. Francis.
(Oxford: Luttrell Society, 1956). The catalogue was published anonymously in 1680–81. It shows that at the height of the frenzy over
the Plot pamphlets were appearing about one a week.

Muddiman, J. G. *The King's Journalist: Studies in the Reign of Charles II.* London: Bodley Head, 1923. Muddiman wrote two weeklies which lasted until 1663, at which time the free press was restricted by the Licensing Act which had been enacted the previous year. Roger L'Estrange, who was appointed Surveyor of the Press, had a monopoly on publishing news. In 1665, however, Muddiman started the *Oxford Gazette*, which lasted for thirteen years and caused L'Estrange to abandon his pro-government news publications. In its format, the *Oxford Gazette* was the precursor of modern newspapers.

Ogg, David. *England in the Reign of Charles II.* 2 vols. Oxford: Clarendon Press, 1956. This is a standard and authoritative work.

Pepys, Samuel. *Diary.* Edited by H. B. Wheatley. 10 vols. New York: Limited Editions Club, 1942. Under the editorship of W. M. Matthews and R. Latham, the University of California Press is now issuing the diary complete and unexpurgated.

Pinto, V. de Sola. *Sir Charles Sedley: 1639–1701. A Study in the Life and Literature of the Restoration.* London: Constable, 1927. This is useful for a view of the Court Wits who, according to Edward Thompson, patronized Oldham.

Pollock, John. *The Popish Plot: A Study in the History of the Reign of Charles II.* Cambridge: Cambridge University Press, 1944. Book presents a carefully researched and balanced view of the Plot by a distinguished lawyer and jurist.

Wedgewood, C. V. *Poetry and Politics Under the Stuarts.* Cambridge: Cambridge University Press, 1961. Study presents a view of the interrelationships of literature and politics during an exciting age.

Wood, Anthony. *Athenae Oxonienses.* 4 vols. Edited by Philip Bliss. London: J. C. and F. Rivington, London: 1813–20.

———. *The Life and Times of Anthony Wood, Antiquary of Oxford, 1632–1695, Described by Himself.* 5 vols. Edited by Andrew Clark. Oxford: Clarendon Press, 1894. The first of these is a biographical dictionary of Oxford alumni; the second, a collection of autobiographical materials and miscellaneous works. Wood, a discontented Oxford scholar, was fond of the caustic remark, as his comments on Oldham show. Despite his inaccuracy and asperity, he, along with John Aubrey, is one of the developers of the biographic sketch as a literary form.

Index